85 -1994

ONSHIP
EYBALL
DRILLS:

mplex Training

CHAMPIONSHIP VOLLEYBALL DRILLS

Volume 2 — Combination and Complex Training

Edited by
Bob Bertucci
Tina Kogut Bertucci

LEISURE PRESS

A publication of
Leisure Press
P.O. Box 3; West Point, N.Y. 10996

ISBN: 88011-035-X
Cover design: Brian Groppe

CONTENTS

PREFACE

The growth of volleyball in the United States, particularly in recent years, has been phenomenal. This growth is reflected by the ever-increasing number of teams representing recreational programs, elementary schools, junior high schools, high schools, colleges, universities, and USVBA programs.

Volleyball drills can generally be grouped into three classifications—simple, combination, and complex. *Championship Volleyball Drills* is a three-volume set. Volume 1 covers simple drills. Volume 2 includes drills for combination and complex training. Volume 3, entitled *The Volleyball Games Book,* presents games that can be played to develop specific volleyball skills. The following chart illustrates the breakdown of drills into three categories.

Drill Categories

	Simple	Combination	Complex
Repetition	One repetition of one skill.	One repetition of two or more skills in a drill, not in succession.	One repetition of two or more skills performed in succession.
	Multiple repetitions of one skill in succession.	Multiple repetitions of each skill in succession, two or more skills in a drill.	Multiple repetitions of two or more skills performed in succession.

The importance of drills cannot be overemphasized. A coach cannot expect a player to execute a skill if that skill has not been learned through adequate practice. In volleyball it is critical that the athlete practice his skills until the movements become automatic. There is simply not adequate time to evoke the conscious cognitive process; the athlete must rely on reaction. Much practice, with planned progression from simple to complex situations, is necessary to achieve such automatic reactions.

Championship Volleyball Drills: Volume 2—Combination and Complex Training is designed to provide you, the coach, with a wide variety of drills from which to select and plan effective teaching and practice sessions. This volume briefly reviews the one-skill simple drill, then moves on to cover the combination and complex drills of both single and multiple repetitions. The drills are organized first by number of skills involved; second by whether it is a simple, combination, or complex drill; and third by whether it is a single or multiple repetition drill.

Because of the tremendous involvement of some of our finest United States coaches, an extensive number of drills has been accumulated. Many of the drills are originals. Most have been gathered and revised over the years as a result of interaction between these contributors and other great teachers, coaches, and clinicians from all over the world. We hope these drills will help you develop your championship volleyball team.

1

ONE-SKILL DRILLS

Accu-Speed Serving Drill

Contributor: Bonnie Kenny
University of Tennessee

Purpose: A pressure drill for serving. Accuracy and repetition of correct serving mechanics are its focus.

Key:

Coach   Ⓧ

Server   Ⓢ

Shagger   Ⓢⓗ

Ball Cart   ⌗

Path of Ball   – – – →

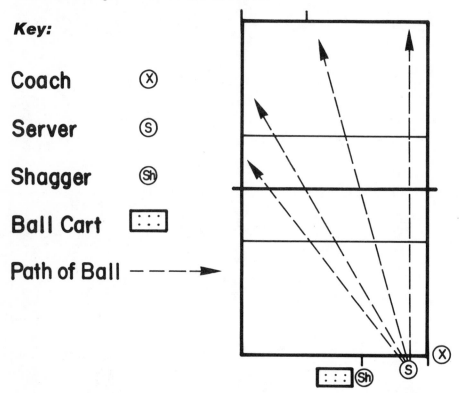

Explanation: The coach sets a one- to two-minute time limit. One player stands on the end line in the serving position. Other players are shagging balls so that the server has a constant supply. The coach stands near the server, timing and counting how many consecutive serves the player achieves in the given amount of time. Once the server misses, a new player replaces the server.

Variations:
1. Require the server to serve to a specific area.
2. Award point values: 3 points for a tough serve to the correct area; 2 points for a legal serve to the correct area; 1 point for a legal serve.

Repeated Setting Drill

Contributor: Ann E. Meyers
University of Dayton

Purpose: To practice overhand passing a variety of tosses; conditioning.

Key:

Coach   (X)

Player   ◯

Setter/Target   ●

Player
New Position   ◌

Shagger   (Sh)

Path of Player ⟶

Path of Ball - - - ➤

Ball Cart   ⬚

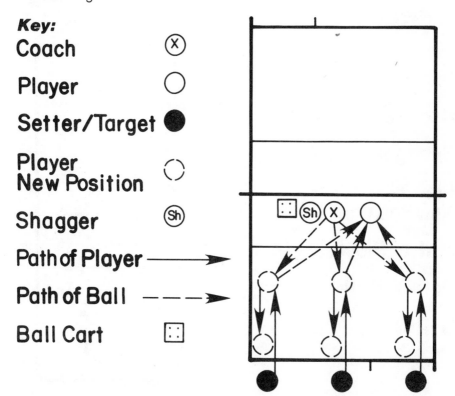

Explanation: The coach tosses a ball to midcourt. The first player moves forward from the baseline and sets to the target. While this player sets, the coach tosses another ball and the next player moves to midcourt to set to the target. While the second player sets, the next setter moves to midcourt to set the third toss from the coach. After setting, each player moves back to the baseline and immediately returns for the next tossed ball.

Variations:
1. Vary the height of the tosses.
2. Have players touch the wall instead of the backline to increase conditioning.

Bread-and-Butter Drill

Contributor: Ralph Hippolyte
French National Volleyball Team

Purpose: To teach backcourt setting.

Key:

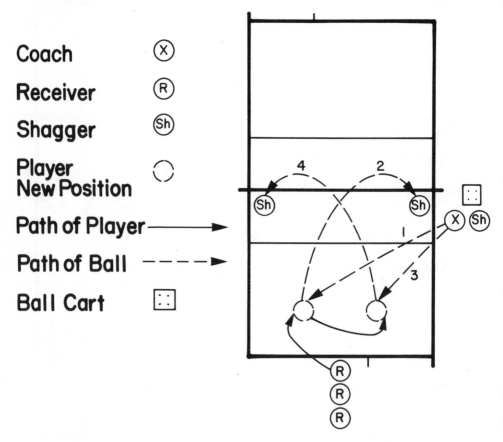

Coach   (X)

Receiver   (R)

Shagger   (Sh)

Player
New Position   ○

Path of Player ——————▶

Path of Ball - - - - ▶

Ball Cart   ⊡

Explanation: The coach tosses a deep ball to the left back (#5) position. The first receiver runs, gets in position behind the ball, and sets a high ball to the right front (#2) position. The coach then tosses a deep ball to the right back (#1) position. The same receiver runs to get in position behind the ball and sets a high ball to the left front (#4) position. The player then returns to the end of the line and the next receiver starts. Continue until time expires or a specific number of repetitions are completed.

Variable Spiking Drill

Contributor: Mario Treibitch
Puerto Rican Women's National Team

Purpose: To train players to spike balls being tossed from different positions and varying speeds and trajectories.

Key:

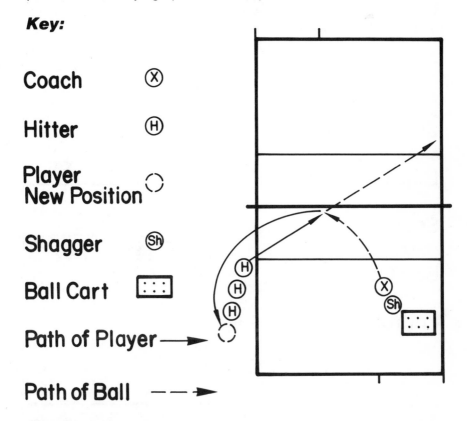

Coach ⊗

Hitter Ⓗ

Player
New Position ◌

Shagger Ⓢⓗ

Ball Cart ⬚

Path of Player ⟶

Path of Ball -- ➤

Explanation: The coach positions himself away from the net. There are three hitters per group. The coach tosses the ball to the left front (#4) position, using varying speeds and trajectories. The hitters must adjust the length and speed of their aproach to successfully position themselves to spike. After they spike they quickly move to the end of the line. The drill continues for a set number of spikes or set amount of time.

Variations:
1. Run the same drill to the right front (#2) position.
2. Vary the positions from which the coach tosses.

Endurance Blocking Drill

Contributor: Marilyn McReavy
University of Florida

Purpose: To emphasize proper movement and blocking skill even as a player experiences fatigue. Works on jumping endurance. Develops determination as well as allows the coach to analyze players' movements and skills easily.

Key:

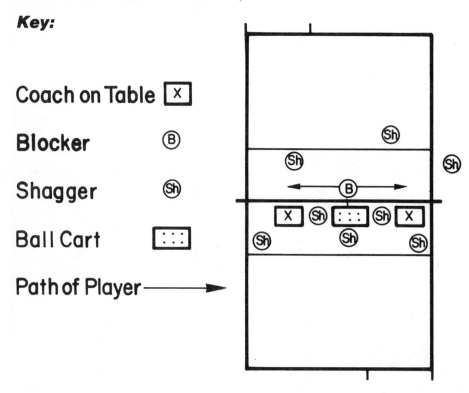

Coach on Table [X]

Blocker Ⓑ

Shagger ⓈⒽ

Ball Cart [⋮]

Path of Player ⟶

Explanation: The blocker moves from one position to the other and attempts to block the ball hit at him. The coach should begin by hitting at the blocker. Emphasize correct footwork. Eliminate incorrect skill even if the drill must go slowly at first. Do not allow bad habits to develop, such as jumping sideways, hitting the net, or stepping back from or under the net.

Variations:
1. Use sidestep, turn-and-run, or crossover step.
2. Progress from hitting at the blocker to hitting around or away.

Juggle Drill

Contributor: Ed Halik
U.S. Air Force Academy

Purpose: To develop ball control and communication.

Key:

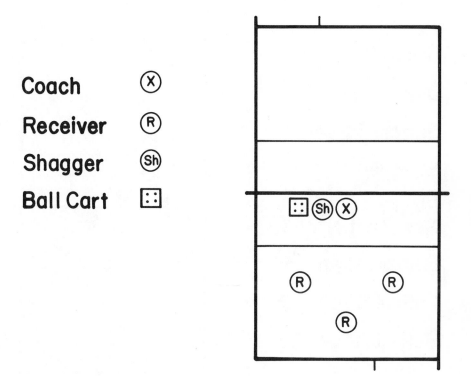

Coach   (X)

Receiver   (R)

Shagger   (Sh)

Ball Cart   ⬚

Explanation: Receivers start about five feet apart. The coach starts with two balls, and tosses the first to any of the receivers. Before the first ball is returned, the coach tosses the second ball. Players try to keep both balls in play with controlled passing.

Variation:
1. Have players dive or roll every time they touch a ball.

Passing Circuit Drill

Contributor: Ralph Hippolyte
French National Volleyball Team

Purpose: To develop speed and range of players.

Key:

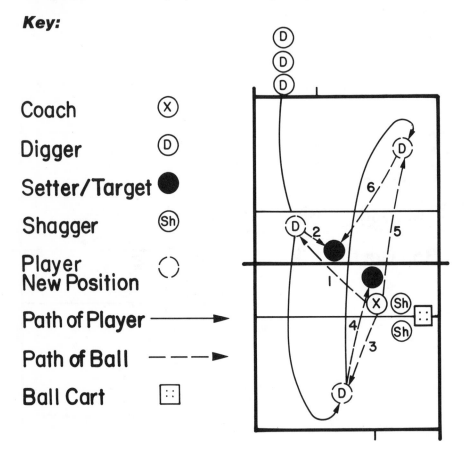

Coach	Ⓧ
Digger	Ⓓ
Setter/Target	●
Shagger	Ⓢⓗ
Player New Position	◯
Path of Player	⟶
Path of Ball	- - - ►
Ball Cart	⊡

Explanation: The coach throws a ball short to the right front (#2) position. The first digger sprints and plays the ball with a roll up to the first target. The same player then sprints under the net to the other side to the left back (#5) position, where the digger digs a spike from the coach to the second target. The player then sprints back under the net to the left back (#5) position and plays a thrown ball from the coach to the first target. Repeat with two more players.

Go-for-Two Drill

Contributor: Bob Bertucci
University of Tennessee

Purpose: To develop the ability to use a dive when playing a ball.

Key:

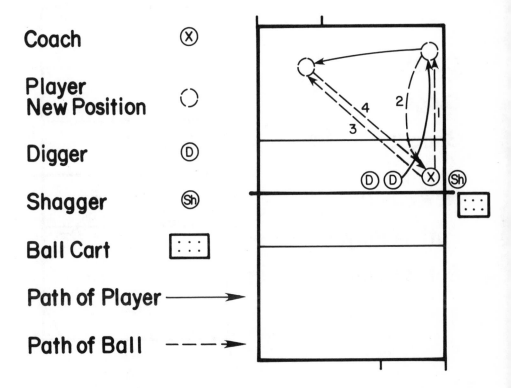

Coach	Ⓧ
Player New Position	⃝
Digger	Ⓓ
Shagger	Ⓢⁱ
Ball Cart	⊡
Path of Player	⟶
Path of Ball	⤍

Explanation: The coach tosses a ball to the left back (#5) position. The first digger must run, dive, and try to play the ball back to the coach. As soon as the first ball is played, the coach tosses the second ball to the right back (#1) position; the same digger dives and tries to play the ball to the coach.

Variation:
1. Have players use a roll to play the ball.

Dig-and-Roll Drill

Contributor: Tina Bertucci
University of Tennessee

Purpose: To practice receiving spikes and executing emergency techniques.

Key:

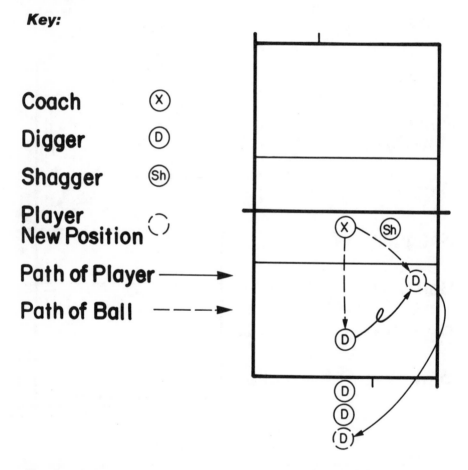

Coach   (X)

Digger   (D)

Shagger   (Sh)

Player
New Position (⌣)

Path of Player ⟶

Path of Ball ⇢

Explanation: The coach spikes a ball at the first digger. As soon as the pass is completed, the coach immediately tosses or spikes another ball at the same digger, who must play it with a roll.

Variations:
1. Work the drill from all backcourt defense positions.
2. Have the coach stand on a table and spike at the players.
3. Have the coach vary attack positions.

The Great Chase Drill

Contributor: Ann E. Meyers
University of Dayton

Purpose: To practice teamwork, communication, and running down a ball that is going out of play.

Key:

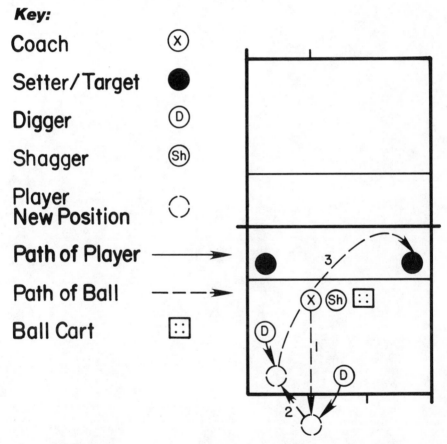

Coach   (X)

Setter/Target   ●

Digger   (D)

Shagger   (Sh)

Player
New Position   ◯

Path of Player   ⟶

Path of Ball   ⇢

Ball Cart   ⊡

Explanation: The coach slaps the ball and tosses a high ball outside the court. On the slap, the two defensive players turn and sprint toward the ball. The closest player calls it and passes back to the other player, who is following. This player passes to either target. Continue the drill until 10 balls have been passed to the targets.

Variations:
1. Work the drill from the right- and center-back defense positions.
2. Have the targets spike the ball.

2

TWO-SKILL DRILLS

Pass or Come Out to Serve Drill

Contributor: Katrinka Jo Crawford
Lamar University

Purpose: To work on passing accuracy, concentrating on serve receive, opening lanes, and moving to the ball.

Key:

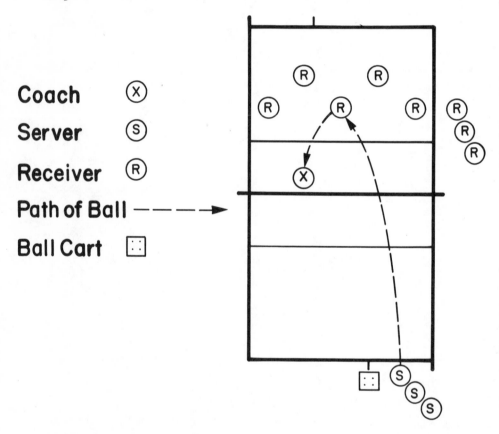

Coach   (X)

Server   (S)

Receiver   (R)

Path of Ball   — — — ➔

Ball Cart   [::]

Explanation: The server serves to the receivers. If the pass is good, the receivers rotate. If the pass is not good, the player committing the error comes out to serve, and the player waiting on the sideline replaces the passer. If the ball hits the floor, all players around the ball come out and are replaced by servers. Each good pass earns the receiver 1 point. The drill continues until one player gets 15 points.

Receiving Carousel Drill

Contributor: Frank Fristensky
Eastern Michigan University

Purpose: To train serving and serve receiving skills.

Key:

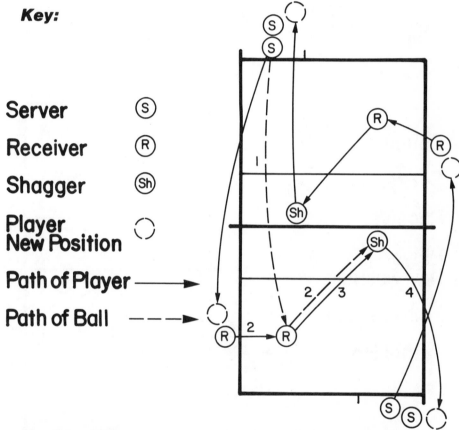

Server   (S)

Receiver   (R)

Shagger   (Sh)

Player
New Position   ◯

Path of Player   ———▶

Path of Ball   — — —▶

Explanation: A server from each service area serves to a receiver. After the serve, both servers run to their new positions and prepare to be the next receiver. Meanwhile, the receiver passes the ball to a shagger in the target area, then runs to the target area to shag the next receiver's pass. The shagger retrieves the pass and goes to the end of the serving line.

Variations:
1. Add a second receiver.
2. Have the target become a setter, who will set to a shagger and eventually to a spiker.
3. Vary receivers' positions.

Players vs. Coach Serve and Receive Drill

Contributor: Tina Bertucci
University of Tennessee

Purpose: To practice serving and passing accuracy.

Key:

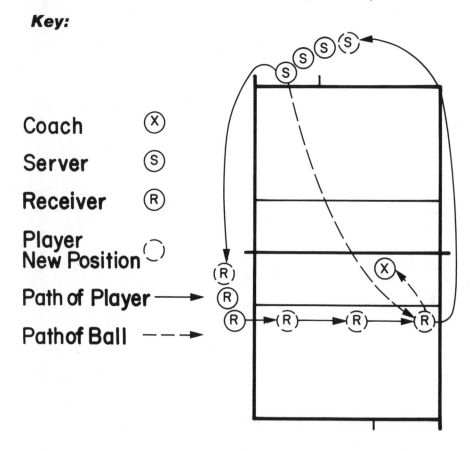

Coach — (X)

Server — (S)

Receiver — (R)

Player New Position — ( )

Path of Player ⟶

Path of Ball – – –▶

Explanation: The first server serves one ball. The receivers try to pass the ball accurately to the coach. After each serve, the receivers move one position to the right. The first server replaces the receiver waiting on the side of the court. The receiver rotating out goes to the serving line. Players receive 1 point for every pass to the coach. The coach receives 1 point for each missed pass or for a missed serve. Play the game to 15 points.

Bread-and-Butter Attack Drill

Contributor: Tina Bertucci
University of Tennessee

Purpose: To practice backcourt setting.

Key:

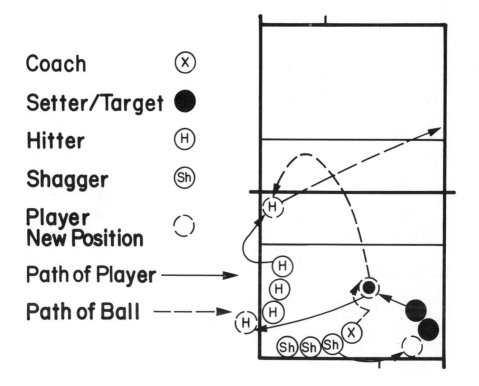

Coach	(X)
Setter/Target	●
Hitter	(H)
Shagger	(Sh)
Player New Position	◌
Path of Player	—————▶
Path of Ball	– – –▶

Explanation: The coach bounces a ball so that it rebounds high in midcourt. The first setter moves quickly under the ball and sets high outside to the first hitter. Rotate positions on every play.

Variations:
1. Run the drill from the opposite corner.
2. Have the passer cover the hitter.
3. Use two lines of hitters, and have passers come from both backcourt positions so that they must communicate who will pass.

Find-the-Hitter Drill

Contributor: Ralph Hippolyte
French National Volleyball Team

Purpose: To develop perfect timing betwen setters and quick hitters; spatial orientation training.

Key:

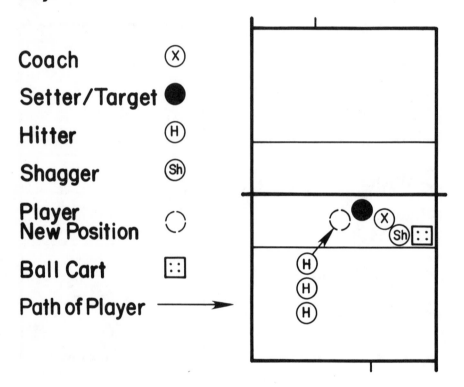

Coach (X)

Setter/Target ●

Hitter (H)

Shagger (Sh)

Player New Position ◯

Ball Cart ▦

Path of Player ⟶

Explanation: The setter is blindfolded, and the coach places a ball in the setter's hands. The first hitter approaches and, when the hitter's arms begin swinging upward, the hitter calls for the ball. The setter sets a quick ball for the hitter to spike. Continue with the remaining hitters.

Variation:
1. Move the setter a specific number of steps in various directions, and have the setter find the hitters, who are driving to a predetermined spot.

Continuous Dig-and-Set Drill

Contributor: Tina Bertucci
University of Tennessee

Purpose: To practice digging accuracy, movement to the ball, and setting.

Key:

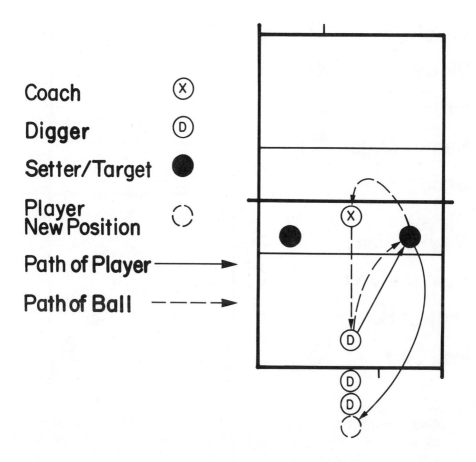

Coach	Ⓧ
Digger	Ⓓ
Setter/Target	⬤
Player New Position	◌
Path of Player	⟶
Path of Ball	----➤

Explanation: The coach spikes at the first digger, who passes to either setter. The setter sets to the coach, who immediately spikes at the next digger. Each digger replaces the setter who received the pass, and the setter moves to the digging line.

Three Corner Drill

Contributor: Nancy Owen Fortner
Loyola Marymount University

Purpose: To warm up for digging and setting, and to teach communication between players, control, and concentration.

Key:

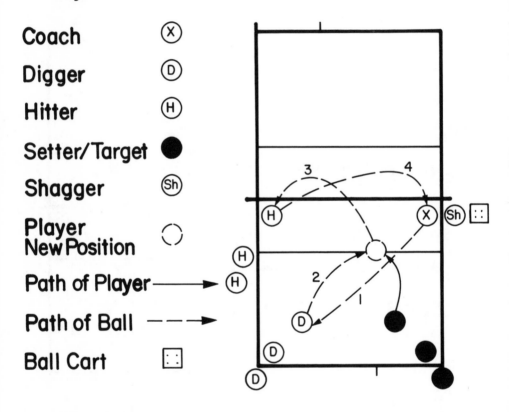

Coach   (X)

Digger   (D)

Hitter   (H)

Setter/Target   ●

Shagger   (Sh)

Player New Position   ◌

Path of Player ⟶

Path of Ball - - ⟶

Ball Cart   ⊡

Explanation: The coach starts the drill by hitting to the first digger in line. The digger passes toward the target area. The first setter penetrates and sets the ball to the spiker. The spiker in turn sets the ball back to the coach, who hits to the next digger in line. Each player rotates clockwise to the next line. Players in line should always be alert to help out.

Variation:
1. The coach can hit from the other side.

Back Attack Drill

Contributor: Barbara L. Viera
University of Delaware

Purpose: To develop quick movement off the net in free ball situations; to practice backsetting and weak-side hitting.

Key:

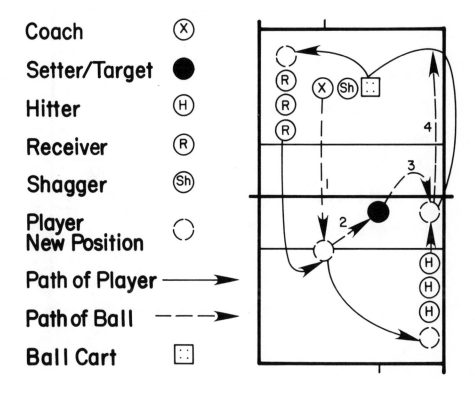

Coach	(X)
Setter/Target	●
Hitter	(H)
Receiver	(R)
Shagger	(Sh)
Player New Position	◯
Path of Player	⟶
Path of Ball	--→
Ball Cart	⊡

Explanation: The coach tosses the ball high over the net. The receiver on the coach's side runs under the net and overhand passes to the setter. The setter backsets to the right front (#2) position and the hitter spikes either down the line or crosscourt. The hitter then shags the ball and goes to the end of the receiving line. Continue the drill for a set time limit or a specific number of good attacks.

Serve and Two Player Receive Drill

Contributor: Linda J. Wambach
University of Evansville

Purpose: To practice deep serves and backcourt receiving.

Key:

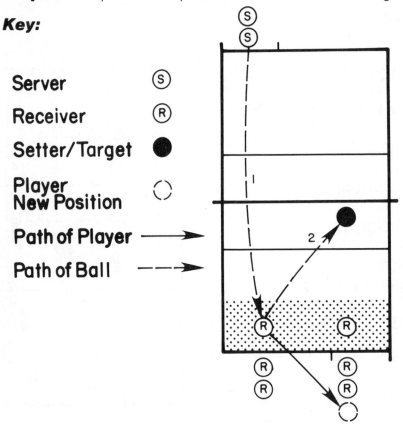

Server   (S)

Receiver   (R)

Setter/Target   ●

Player
New Position   ○

Path of Player   ⟶

Path of Ball   ‒‒⟶

Explanation: The server serves to the shaded area. One of the two receivers calls the ball and passes to the target area. The other receiver remains on the court until a pass is attempted. The passing receiver goes to the end of the other receiving line. A receiver goes to the end of the serving line after passing to the target area twice; the server replaces that receiver at the end of the appropriate receiving line. The server shags the ball and hustles back to the serving line.

Variation:
1. Add a setter in the target area to set every pass.

Three-Player Line Serve and Receive Drill

Contributor: Tina Bertucci
University of Tennessee

Purpose: To work on serve and serve receive accuracy.

Key:

Server   (S)

Receiver   (R)

Shagger   (Sh)

Path of Ball - - - →

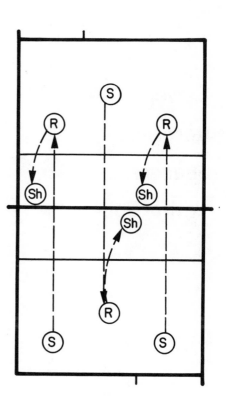

Explanation: The servers serve straight ahead to the receivers, who pass to their targets. Players rotate positions within their groups after a prescribed number of serves. Use two balls per group to keep the drill moving quickly.

Variations:
1. If players cannot serve accurately, have them toss the ball over the net.
2. Move servers back behind the baseline.

Target Passing Drill

Contributor: Ralph Hippolyte
French National Volleyball Team

Purpose: To train serve and serve receive accuracy.

Key:

Server   ⓢ

Receiver   ⓡ

Shagger   ⓢⱨ

Path of Ball   - - - - →

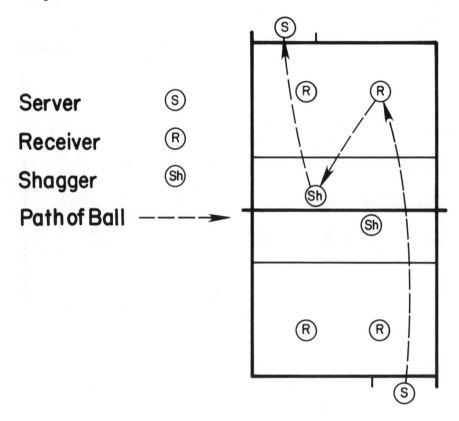

Explanation: The targets and servers begin with one ball each. The servers serve to the left back (#5) position and the right back (#1) position. The receivers pass the balls to their respective targets. As soon as the servers serve, the targets roll the next ball to their server. After 10 serves, rotate so that the server plays position #1, position #1 moves to position #5, position #5 moves to target, and the target becomes the server.

Triangle Serve-Receive Drill

Contributor: Chris S. Wyman
Northeastern University

Purpose: To improve passing accuracy and communication in service reception.

Key:

Server   (S)

Receiver   (R)

Target   ●

Path of Ball — — →

Explanation: Each server alternately serves 15 balls aiming for the center front, right, or left back receiving positions. Receivers try to pass to the target, rotating after three serves. The serving group counts the number of good serves, and the receivers count the number of good passes. The group with the highest total of good serves and good passes wins.

Variations:
1. Move receivers to the left front, center front, and left back positions.
2. Move receivers to the right front, center front, and right back positions.
3. Have the nonpassing receivers run an attack combination.

Shambaugh Library

Jumpsetter Drill

Contributor: John Blair
University of Tennessee

Purpose: To work the setter's options as an attacker/setter in 5-1 offensive situations.

Key:

Coach	Ⓧ
Setter	●
Hitter	Ⓗ
Shagger	Ⓢⓗ
Player New Position	◌
Path of Player	⟶
Path of Ball	⇢
Ball Cart	⊡

Explanation: The coach tosses a ball to the zone at the net from which the offense is to be initiated. Tosses should allow the setter to jumpset all balls. An attacker should be positioned to spike from either the right, middle, or left front (#2, 3, or 4) positions. As the toss is made, the setter begins moving to the ball. Simultaneously, the attacker calls the set desired and positions herself to approach. The setter then adjusts to the tossed ball and either jumps and sets to the hitter or attacks on the second contact.

Variations:
1. Add blockers to the drill.
2. Use a player instead of the coach's toss to pass.

Watch-the-Spiker Blocking Drill

Contributor: Doug Beal
USA Men's National Team

Purpose: To train the blockers to watch the spiker during the block. Also used to train blocking form.

Key:

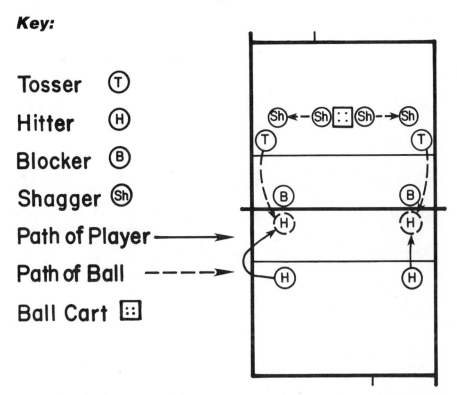

Tosser Ⓣ

Hitter Ⓗ

Blocker Ⓑ

Shagger ⓢⓗ

Path of Player ⎯⎯⎯→

Path of Ball ⎯ ⎯ ⎯→

Ball Cart ▣

Explanation: A blocker is situated on the opposite side of the net from the spiker. The tosser tosses a ball from behind the blocker to the spiker, who approaches and spikes. The blocker must watch the spiker to get the visual cues needed to block the ball. The spiker quickly transitions off the net to spike again. The drill continues until the blocker has blocked a specified number of balls, then the two players switch positions.

Variations:
1. Have the tosser toss slightly to the right or left, forcing the blocker to adjust.
2. Use two blockers.

Team Blocking Recovery Drill

Contributor: Mike Wilton
University of Washington

Purpose: To develop an awareness of hitter coverage/block recovery, to teach "watch the block" principle, and to improve transition/reaction time.

Key:

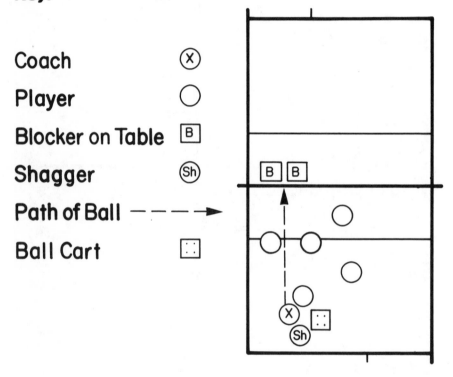

Coach	Ⓧ
Player	◯
Blocker on Table	B
Shagger	Sh
Path of Ball	– – – ➔
Ball Cart	⬚

Explanation: The coach tosses a ball at the blockers, who are standing on a box or table. The blockers bat the ball to different areas of the court. Players, executing spiker coverage, must retrieve the ball.

Variations:
1. Run an attack off spiker coverage.
2. The coach spikes at two blockers who are jumping from the floor.

Center-Switch Three-Player "D" Drill

Contributor: Debbie Sokol
Rice University

Purpose: To practice backcourt defense, filling in vacant areas, and backcourt setting.

Key:

Coach   Ⓧ

Digger   Ⓓ

Shagger   ⓢⓗ

Player
New Position   ◌

Path of Player ⟶

Path of Ball – – – ▸

Ball Cart   ⊡

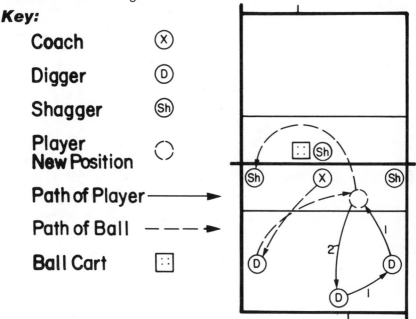

Explanation: The coach spikes at any one of the three diggers. The digger then passes the ball toward the target area. The player opposite the digger sets the ball, wherever it is passed, high outside and in the direction she is facing. (For example, if the player in left back (#5) position passes the ball, the player in right back (#1) position sets to left front (#4) position. If the player in center back (#6) position passes the ball, the player in #1 position again sets. If the digger is the player in #1 position, the player in #5 position sets to the right front (#2) position.) The #6 position shifts to cover the position vacated by whoever set the ball. The player setting then returns to #6 position after delivering the ball. This drill continues for a set time or for a goal determined by the coach.

Variations:
1. The coach can be located anyplace at the net.
2. Instead of shagging the set balls, set the balls back to the coach and continue the drill.

Four-Player Setting Drill

Contributor: Lucy Ticki
Seton Hall University

Purpose: To develop control of overhand passing and to build quick movement patterns.

Key:

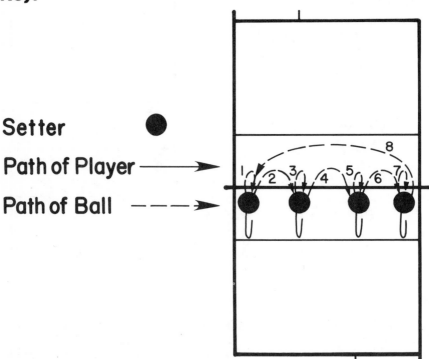

Setter

Path of Player ———→

Path of Ball —— —→

Explanation: Four players line up along the net. The player in the left front (#4) position begins with a self-set, then sets to the second player who in turn self-sets, turns under the ball, and sets to the third player. The third player repeats the sequence. The fourth player self-sets, then sets the length of the net back to the #4 position. During the drill, after each player has set to the next player in line, he must dive, touch the attack line, and return to set the ball again. Continue the drill for one minute, then rotate positions.

Variations:
1. Run the drill using both sides of the net.
2. Instead of diving, run and touch the attack line.

Four Corners Drill

Contributor: Richard Scott
University of Montana

Purpose: To develop defensive reactions.

Key:

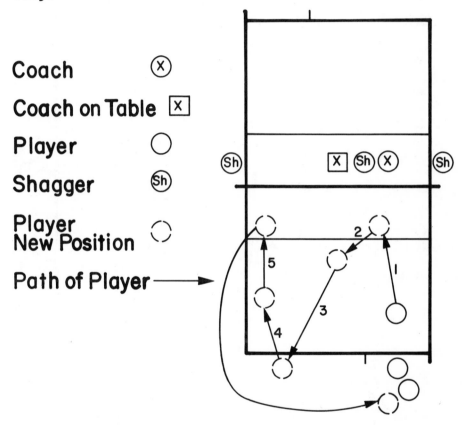

Coach   Ⓧ

Coach on Table   ☒

Player   ◯

Shagger   ⓢₕ

Player
New Position   ◌

Path of Player ⟶

Explanation: The coach stands on a table and runs one player at a time through the following sequence: Start with a dig; 1) pick up a tip; 2) set a ball to the left front (#4) position; 3) run a ball down; 4) dig a spike; 5) pick up a tip. As soon as the first player in each group is finished, the next should be ready to go. Use groups of threes with each player going through five times.

Hustle Up Drill

Contributor: Cathy Fulford
Brown University

Purpose: To develop digging skills, acceleration to play balls, and transition to spiking.

Key:

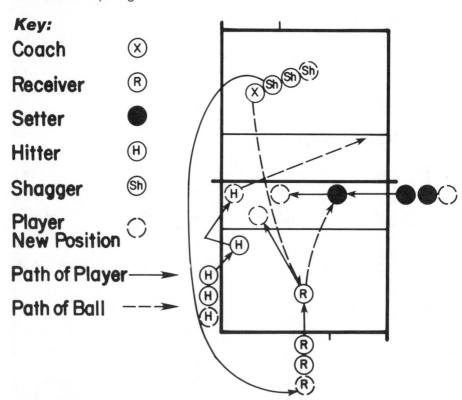

Coach   Ⓧ

Receiver   Ⓡ

Setter   ●

Hitter   Ⓗ

Shagger   Ⓢⁿ

Player New Position   ◌

Path of Player ⟶

Path of Ball --→

Explanation: The coach is situated at center court near the net. The coach spikes a hard driven ball toward the player in the left back (#5) position, requiring proper execution of a dig. Immediately after the dig, the coach tosses a ball to be spiked to the left front (#4) position. As soon as the player lands, a ball is thrown into the right back (#1) position, which the player must run to and play back to a target. Upon recovering from executing an emergency technique, another ball is tossed high in the right front (#2) position, which the player must attack dink. The circuit is completed once the player has run around the outside of the court to the end of the line. The drill is continuous and each player completes a prescribed number of trips.

Variations:
1. Run the same drill, starting on the opposite side of the court.
2. Increase the difficulty of the drill by requiring each defensive pass to go to the target.

Power Digging and Hitting Drill

Contributor: Lucy Ticki
Seton Hall University

Purpose: To practice good passes to the setter from a hard driven spike, to build quick movement patterns, and to strengthen hitting ability.

Key:

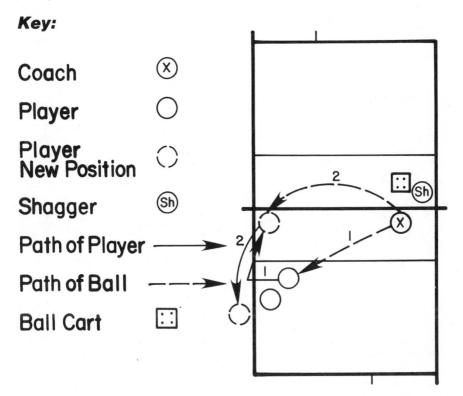

Coach   (X)

Player   O

Player New Position   (dashed circle)

Shagger   (Sh)

Path of Player   ———→

Path of Ball   – – –→

Ball Cart   (cart symbol)

Explanation: From the right front (#2) position, the coach hits a hard driven spike to the first player then tosses a high ball close to the net for the same player to spike. After the spike, the player runs to the end of the line. Continue the drill for two minutes before changing groups.

Variations:
1. Add a setter to set the dug ball.
2. Run the drill from the left front (#4) position.
3. Add a blocker.
4. Vary the types of sets.

Block Exchange Drill

Contributor: Jerry Angle
Northwestern University

Purpose: To develop double-blocking technique, to give spikers a chance to hit against a double block, and to develop endurance.

Key:

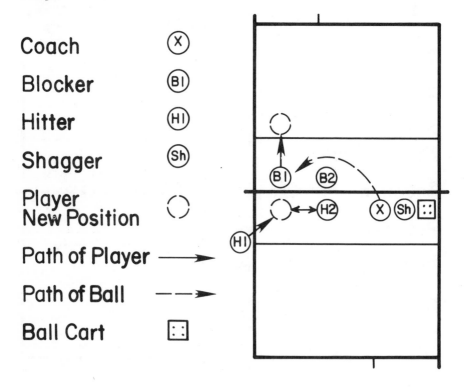

Coach   (X)

Blocker   (BI)

Hitter   (HI)

Shagger   (Sh)

Player
New Position   ( )

Path of Player ⟶

Path of Ball --->

Ball Cart ⊡

Explanation: The coach tosses a ball to H1, who spikes against the opposing blockers. After the hit, H1 and H2 exchange positions and get in position to block. B1 backs off the net and the coach tosses another ball over the net for B1 to hit. H1 and H2 attempt to block the hit. After the hit, B1 and B2 exchange positions and H2 backs off the net to hit against the block. Players always exchange positions after their side hits. The drill continues for 25 tosses.

Block Recovery Drill

Contributor: Tina Bertucci
University of Tennessee

Purpose: To practice coming off a block and playing a ball, and to develop teamwork and communication.

Key:

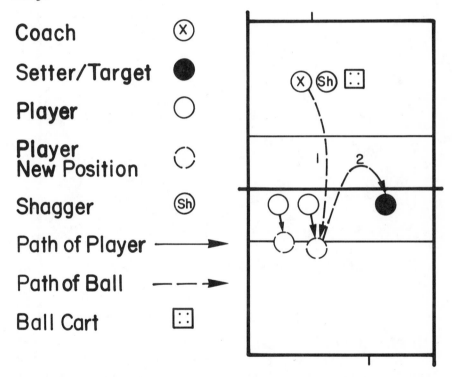

Coach	Ⓧ
Setter/Target	⬤
Player	◯
Player New Position	◌
Shagger	(Sh)
Path of Player	⟶
Path of Ball	-- ➤
Ball Cart	⊡

Explanation: The coach slaps the ball, then tosses the ball within the zone of the blockers' coverage. On the slap, the players block, turn, and step toward the ball. The player closest to the ball calls it and passes it to the target. Continue the drill until 10 balls have been passed to the target.

Variations:
1. Run the drill from the middle and right front positions.
2. Have one of the blockers spike the ball.
3. Have the target spike the ball.

Blocker-to-Hitter Transition Drill

Contributor: Mike English University of Missouri

Purpose: To train blockers to make the transition to offense as a hitter.

Key:

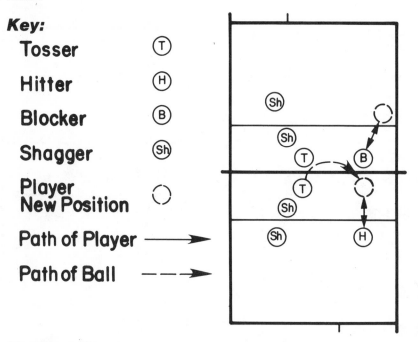

Tosser	Ⓣ
Hitter	Ⓗ
Blocker	Ⓑ
Shagger	(Sh)
Player New Position	◯
Path of Player	⟶
Path of Ball	--⟶

Explanation: A tossed (or set) ball is spiked by the hitter as another player tries to block. The blocker then moves off the net and prepares to hit a tossed (or set) ball while the first hitter prepares to block. This sequence continues until a player has blocked three balls. Then the next player in line hits the next ball and continues the drill. Each player should go through the line three times.

Variations:
1. Toss the ball to the setter.
2. Have the players do the drill from the opposite side of the net.
3. After the third block, have the players turn and play a tossed ball for the second contact.
4. Have the coach hit at the blocker from a chair in between spikes by that player.
5. Increase the number of repetitions to work on jump training.

Co-Gema Drill

**Contributor: Cathy Fulford
Brown University**

Purpose: To practice backcourt defense.

Key:

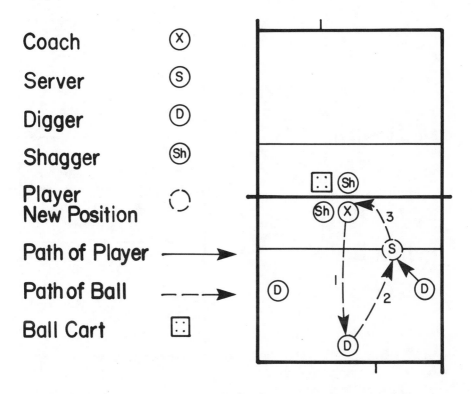

Coach	Ⓧ
Server	Ⓢ
Digger	Ⓓ
Shagger	Ⓢⓗ
Player New Position	⟲
Path of Player	⟶
Path of Ball	⇢
Ball Cart	⊡

Explanation: The coach stands in the middle of the court, close to the net. Diggers play the left back (#1), the center back (#6), and the right back (#5) positions according to their strengths. The coach hits or dinks to any of the three positions. If the player in position #5 or #6 digs, the player in position #1 sets to the coach. If the player in position #1 digs, the player in position #5 sets to the coach.

Variation:
1. The coach hits from the right or left front position.

Balance Drill

Contributor: Merri Dwight
South Bay Spoilers

Purpose: To practice covering the court on defense and reading the hitter.

Key:

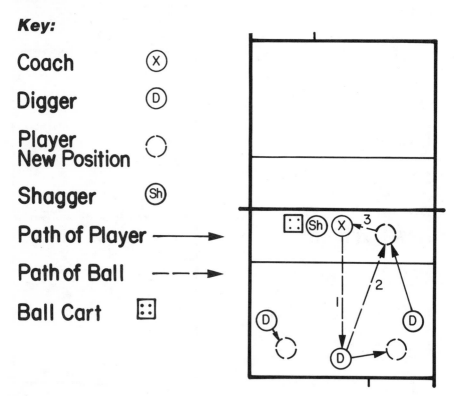

Coach   Ⓧ

Digger   Ⓓ

Player
New Position   ◯

Shagger   ⓢⓗ

Path of Player   ⟶

Path of Ball   ⇢

Ball Cart   ⊡

Explanation: Three diggers start in base defense position, as shown. The coach spikes at any one of the diggers. Depending on where the dig goes, one of the other players must step in and set the ball back to the coach. The remaining two players immediately balance the court (one in each corner 5′ from the sideline and 5′ from the endline). The player who sets stays up for dinks and roll shots. The coach spikes or dinks again and the sequence continues.

Variations:
1. Work both sides of the net.
2. The coach can move to the right front and left front areas of the court.

3

THREE-SKILL DRILLS

Serve, Pass, and Set Drill

Contributor: Veronica Hammersmith
West Virginia University

Purpose: To work on serving, passing, and setting.

Key:

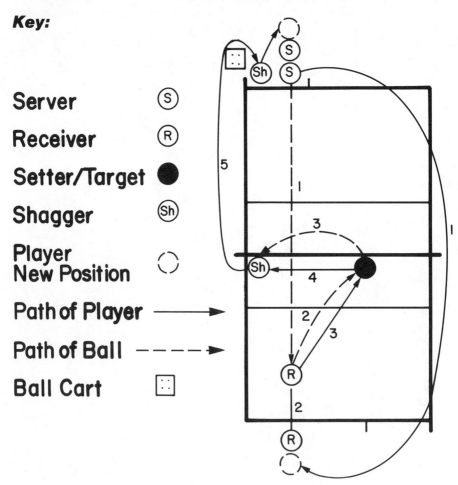

Server (S)

Receiver (R)

Setter/Target ●

Shagger (Sh)

Player
New Position ◯

Path of Player ──────▶

Path of Ball ── ── ──▶

Ball Cart ⊡

Explanation: The server serves to a receiver, who passes to the setter. The setter sets to the left front (#4) position. The ball is caught and returned to a shagger, who gives the ball to the server. Rotate from server, to receiver, to setter, to catcher, to shagger, to server.

Variation:
1. Start receivers at the attack line and serve deep, requiring backward movement before passing.

Combination Pass, Set, Spike, and Cover Drill

Contributor: Tina Bertucci
University of Tennessee

Purpose: To work on passing and setting accuracy, spiking, teamwork, and spiker coverage.

Key:

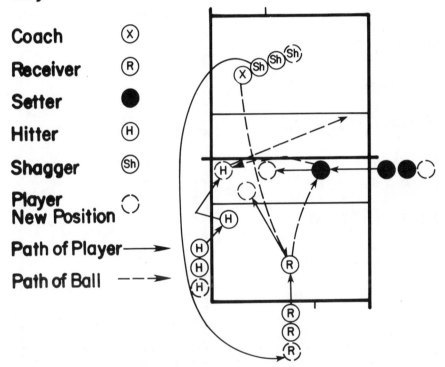

Coach	Ⓧ
Receiver	Ⓡ
Setter	●
Hitter	Ⓗ
Shagger	ⓈⒽ
Player New Position	◌
Path of Player	⟶
Path of Ball	⇢

Explanation: The coach serves to the first receiver. The receiver passes to the setter, who sets a high ball to the hitter in the left front (#4) position. Both the receiver and setter move in to cover the hitter. After spiking, the hitter retrieves the ball and moves to the shagging line. Other players rotate by following the path of the ball.

Variations:
1. Vary the position of the receiving and spiking lines.
2. Vary the type and difficulty of the serves.
3. Add blockers, or have someone toss a ball for spiker coverage.

Assignment Blocking Drill

Contributor: Mary Jo Peppler
University of Florida

Purpose: To teach a blocker in a one-on-one situation to control where opposing spikers can hit the ball; to teach proper body and hand positioning.

Key:

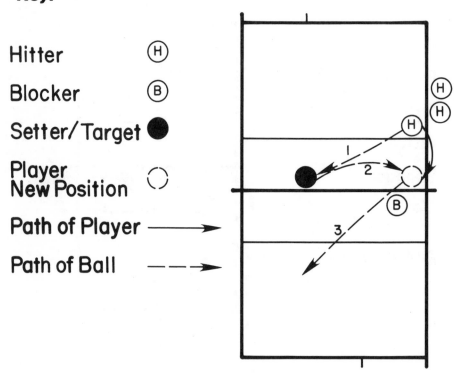

Hitter   Ⓗ

Blocker   Ⓑ

Setter/Target   ●

Player   ◯
New Position   ◠

Path of Player   ⟶

Path of Ball   --→

Explanation: The hitter passes to the setter, who sets to the left front (#4) position. The hitter is directed to spike crosscourt. The blocker must stop this hit.

Variations:
1. Change the hitter's assignment to line.
2. Add diggers (especially to cover the open shot), allowing the spiker to hit any direction.

Block-and-Set Drill

Contributor: Mary Jo Peppler
University of Florida

Purpose: To learn to block and recover to set, reacting to a dug ball; to practice spiking technique (International 4-2 or 5-1 offensive system).

Key:

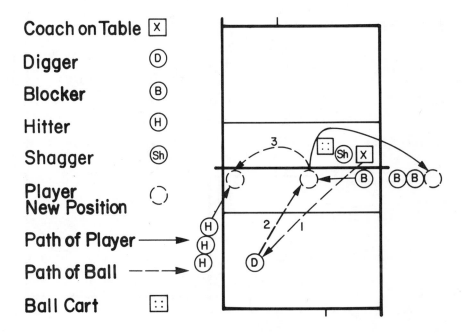

Coach on Table   ⊠

Digger   Ⓓ

Blocker   Ⓑ

Hitter   Ⓗ

Shagger   Ⓢⓗ

Player New Position   ◯

Path of Player ──→

Path of Ball ----→

Ball Cart   ⊡

Explanation: The coach spikes the ball around the blocker toward the defensive player (occasionally spike into the blocker to keep effort at high intensity). The defensive player digs back to the blocker. The blocker sets to the hitter in the left front (#4) position. After each play, the blocker and hitter hustle to the end of their lines, keeping the drill moving quickly.

Variation:
1. Execute the drill from various court positions.

Controlled Dig, Set, and Hit Drill

Contributor: Norman Brandl
University of Texas in El Paso

Purpose: To develop continuity of digging, setting, and hitting.

Key:

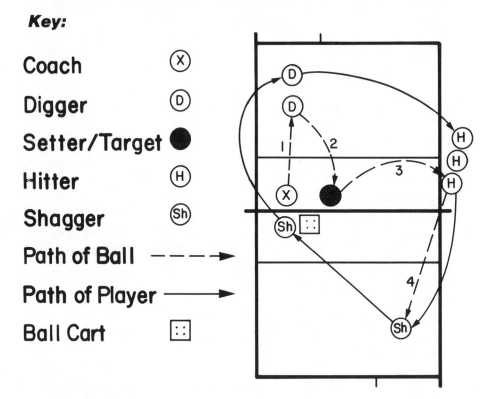

Coach   Ⓧ

Digger   Ⓓ

Setter/Target   ●

Hitter   Ⓗ

Shagger   ⓢʰ

Path of Ball   ‑ ‑ ‑ →

Path of Player   ⟶

Ball Cart   ⊡

Explanation: The coach spikes at a digger, who digs to the setter. The setter must get to the ball and set it to the hitter. The hitter shags the spike and goes to the digging line. The digger goes to the hitting line.

Variations:
1. Have extra athletes shag and do the drill without rotating individually.
2. Add extra setters and have them alternate to increase the speed of the drill.
3. The coach can be at different positions at the net, spiking to the digger at different angles.

Dig, Set, and Hit Drill

Contributor: Katrinka Jo Crawford
Lamar University

Purpose: To practice digging, setting, and hitting skills; teamwork.

Key:

Coach on Table   X

Digger   D

Hitter   H

Setter/Target   ●

Shagger   Sh

Path of Player ——▶

Path of Ball - - -▶

Ball Cart   ⬚

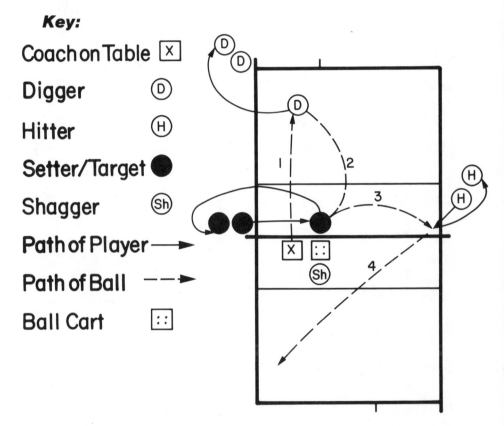

Explanation: The coach hits the ball at the first digger, who passes to the first setter. The setter sets to the left front (#4) position to the first hitter. As soon as the ball is set, the coach hits at the next digger. Players stay in the same groups until the coach has them rotate. Diggers and hitters switch within their respective groups on every play. Setters switch every other play.

Variations:
1. Change the position of the diggers.
2. Change the position of the hitters.
3. Add blockers to the drill.

Bad-Pass Setting Drill

Contributor: Frankie Albitz
Oral Roberts University

Purpose: To teach setting from various positions and under various conditions; to teach hitters and blockers to adjust to sets from various positions on the court.

Key:

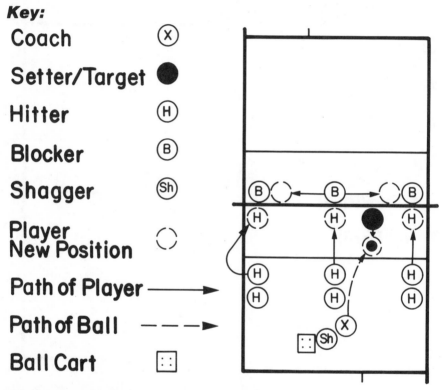

Coach	Ⓧ
Setter/Target	●
Hitter	Ⓗ
Blocker	Ⓑ
Shagger	Ⓢⱨ
Player New Position	◠
Path of Player	──────►
Path of Ball	─ ─ ─►
Ball Cart	⊡

Explanation: The coach stands at midcourt and tosses balls to a setter at the net. The tosses are to various positions on the court and the setter must set every tossed ball. The hitters and blockers adjust to the tosses and the sets. The coach tosses the next ball as soon as the hitter spikes.

Variations:
1. Run setters from behind one of the hitting lines, using more than one setter.
2. Position the coach on the other side of the net and use a player to pass the tossed ball.

Korean Attack Drill
Contributor: Veronica Hammersmith
West Virginia University

Purpose: To work on movement and passing, setting various sets, calling play sets, and running particular combinations.

Key:

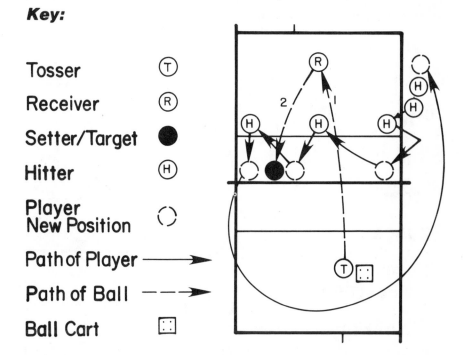

Tosser	(T)
Receiver	(R)
Setter/Target	●
Hitter	(H)
Player New Position	◯
Path of Player	⟶
Path of Ball	⇢
Ball Cart	⬚

Explanation: A receiver in the middle back (#6) position passes the ball to the setter, regardless of where it is thrown. The same receiver passes 5-10 balls in a row or until some objective is reached. The setter sets to one of three spikers. If your team runs particular plays, work on them in the drill. After the ball is spiked, the right-side hitter shags it, returns it to the tosser, and goes to the spiking line. The spiking line rotates to the right on every play.

Variations:
1. Run 5-10 consecutive attack patterns before switching any players.
2. Have the hitter who spikes shag the ball and be immediately replaced.
3. Use two receivers for passing and spiker coverage.

One-on-One Drill

Contributor: Darlene Bailey
Boise State University

Purpose: To work on defensive positioning for a one-player block; to improve the movement of the outside blocker and the middle back; to train the hitter to spike one-on-one.

Key:

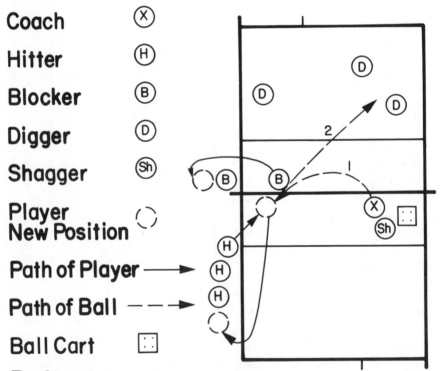

Coach	Ⓧ
Hitter	Ⓗ
Blocker	Ⓑ
Digger	Ⓓ
Shagger	Ⓢⓗ
Player New Position	◯ ⌣
Path of Player	⟶
Path of Ball	— — ⟶
Ball Cart	⊡

Explanation: The coach tosses/sets at fairly rapid intervals. The hitters spike one ball, then rotate clockwise after each hit. The blocker stays and blocks each hitter, then rotates after three attempts. The defense positions itself around the movement of the blocker and tries to touch every ball the hitter spikes or tips. After two minutes, rotate hitters to blockers, blockers to defenders, defenders to shaggers, and shaggers to hitters.

Variations:

1. Move blockers and hitters to middle or right side.
2. Have the coach toss to the setter.

Outside Hit vs. Block Drill

Contributor: Mike Wilton
Cal Poly San Luis Obispo

Purpose: To work outside hitters against blockers, and to practice positioning on an outside block, setting high outside, and conditioning.

Key:

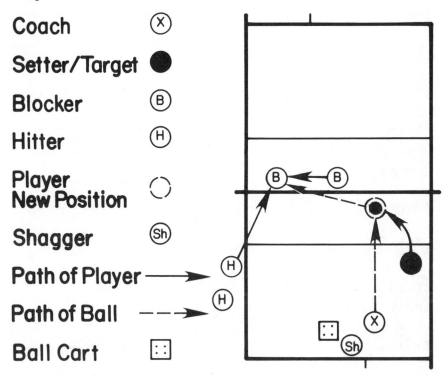

Coach   Ⓧ

Setter/Target ⬤

Blocker   Ⓑ

Hitter   Ⓗ

Player
New Position   ◌

Shagger   Ⓢⓗ

Path of Player ⟶

Path of Ball ⤑

Ball Cart   ⊡

Explanation: The coach tosses or bounces a ball to the setter. The setter penetrates and sets high outside to the hitter, who attacks against the blockers. A preset goal (e.g., 10 balls down) causes a rotation.

Variations:
1. Run the setter from center court.
2. Have hitters and blockers work the other side of the net.
3. Have a second hitter call the open shot.
4. Add a digger.

Hit and "D" Drill

Contributor: Stephanie Schleuder
University of Minnesota

Purpose: To develop the offense's ability to hit around the block and to read the hitter and react to a well-hit spike.

Key:

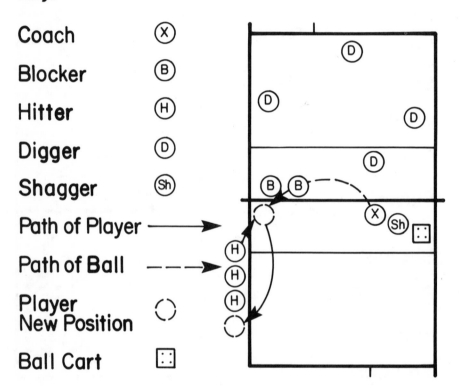

Coach	Ⓧ
Blocker	Ⓑ
Hitter	Ⓗ
Digger	Ⓓ
Shagger	Ⓢⁱ
Path of Player	⟶
Path of Ball	- - ➔
Player New Position	◯
Ball Cart	▦

Explanation: The coach tosses balls continuously to players in the hitting line, who try to hit around the block to score. The defense tries to block or dig each hit. After six balls have been successfully blocked or dug by the defensive group and kept in play, the two groups switch sides of the net.

Variation:
1. Omit block or use only one blocker.

Two-Minute Defense Drill

Contributor: Kay Woodiel
Arkansas State University

Purpose: To train readiness on defense and digging a crosscourt spike.

Key:

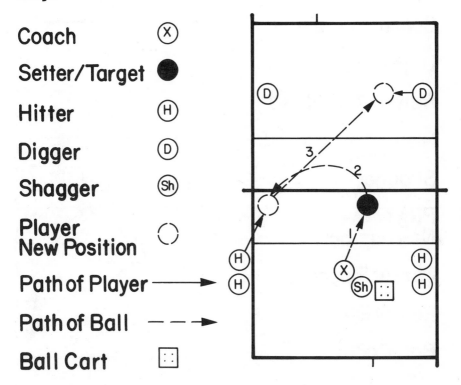

Coach	(X)
Setter/Target	●
Hitter	(H)
Digger	(D)
Shagger	(Sh)
Player New Position	◯
Path of Player	——→
Path of Ball	– – →
Ball Cart	⊡

Explanation: Start with two players on one side of the court, located on or outside the sidelines. The coach tosses a ball to the setter. The setter alternates setting the two attacking lines while the hitters spike near the crosscourt digger. Each digger moves in one at a time to dig a spike, then returns to the sideline. Each pair works for two minutes, changing sides after one minute.

Variations:
1. Start diggers at the baseline and work on defending a down-the-line attack.

Set-the-Dig Drill

Contributor: Judy Mogabgab
University of New Orleans

Purpose: To execute an offense off a dig.

Key:

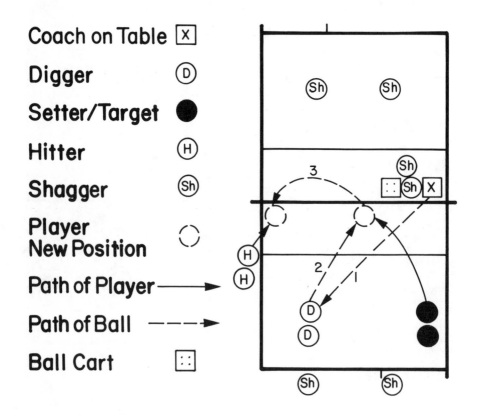

Coach on Table	X
Digger	D
Setter/Target	●
Hitter	H
Shagger	Sh
Player New Position	◯
Path of Player	——→
Path of Ball	––→
Ball Cart	⠿

Explanation: The coach hits to the first digger, who passes to a penetrating setter. The setter sets to the hitter in the left front (#4) position, who spikes anywhere in the court. After 10 good spikes, rotate positions.

Variations:
1. Change the position of the defense.
2. Change the coach's position.
3. Change the position of the hitters.

Transition Setting Drill
Contributor: Jerry Angle
Northwestern University

Purpose: To practice setting a ball that is dug; transition.

Key:

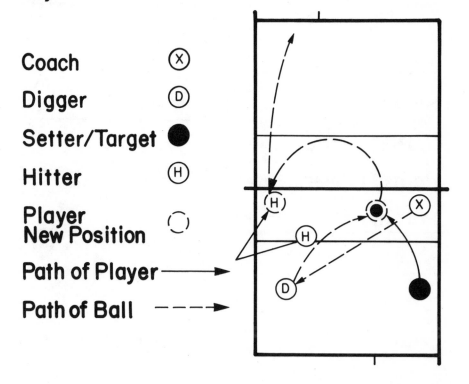

Coach   ⊗

Digger   Ⓓ

Setter/Target   ●

Hitter   Ⓗ

Player
New Position   ◠

Path of Player ⟶

Path of Ball ⤍ ⟶

Explanation: The coach hits at the digger or tips at the hitter, who passes to the target area in the middle or right third of the court along the net. The hitter then gets in position to spike as the setter penetrates to the net and sets to the left front (#4) position. The coach should occasionally hit the ball to the setter to assure that the setter does not release too soon.

Variations:
1. Add blockers.
2. Add a middle back player.

Continuous Volley Drill

Contributor: Ralph Hippolyte
French National Volleyball Team

Purpose: To train ball control and play sequence.

Key:

Receiver (R)

Hitter (H)

Setter ●

Path of Player ———▶

Path of Ball ----▶

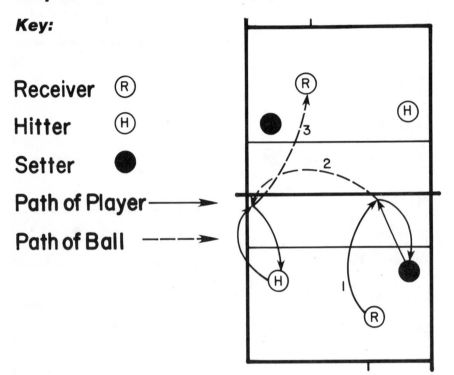

Explanation: The receiver starts the drill by passing to the right front (#2) position. The setter runs in and sets to the left front (#4) position. The hitter runs in and hits over the net to the opposite receiver. This group repeats the sequence. Players must return to beginning positions after each attack. Rotate after completing a specific number of repetitions or once time has expired.

Variations:
1. Have the hitter approach and jumpset to the opposite receiver.
2. Have the hitter approach and tip long or roll shot to the opposite receiver.
3. Have the hitter approach and spike to the opposite receiver.
4. Move the receiver to a different position and attack option.

Ball-Control Sequence Drill

Contributor: Ralph Hippolyte
French National Volleyball Team

Purpose: To train memory, ball control, and play sequence.

Key:

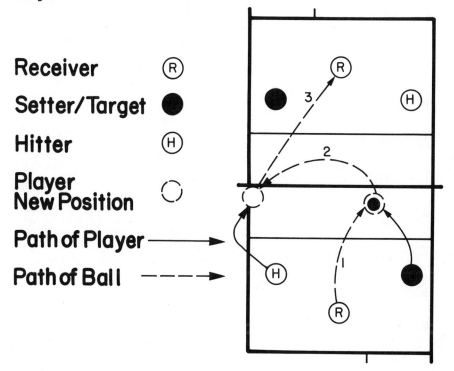

Receiver Ⓡ

Setter/Target ●

Hitter Ⓗ

Player
New Position ◌

Path of Player ⟶

Path of Ball - - - ⟶

Explanation: Either receiver starts the drill by passing to the right front (#2) position. The setter runs in and sets to the left front (#4) position. The hitter approaches and hits to the receiver on the other side. The other side repeats the sequence without stopping the ball. Rotate after completing a specific number of repetitions or once time has expired. Players should always return to base position.

Variation:
1. The hitter can spike approach and jumpset to the opposing receiver.

Killer Drill

Contributor: Tina Bertucci
University of Tennessee

Purpose: To train block, spike, and dig sequence; to develop endurance.

Key:

Coach   Ⓧ

Hitter   Ⓗ

Blocker   Ⓑ

Digger   Ⓓ

Shagger   ⓢⓗ

Path of Player ⟶

Path of Ball ---->

Ball Cart ⬚

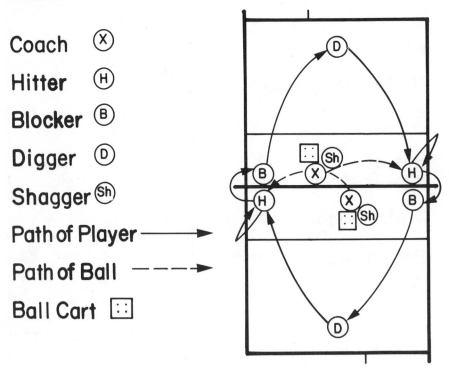

Explanation: The drill begins when all net players jump and block. Then both hitters in the left front (#4) position back off the net and spike a toss from the coach on the same side of the net. Blockers try to stop the hitter across from them, and diggers try to pass if the ball gets past the block. Then all players rotate clockwise and the new spikers step in. The drill continues until every hitter has attempted 10 spikes.

Defensive Circuit Drill

Contributor: Bob Gambardella
United States Military Academy

Purpose: To train defensive play and movement.

Key:

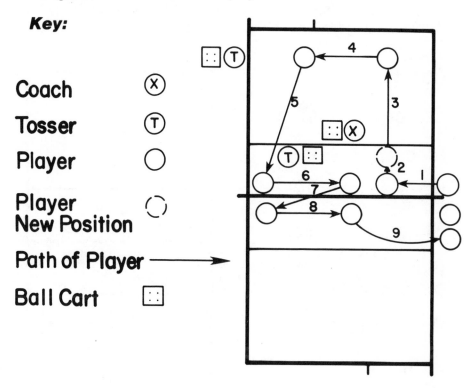

Coach   Ⓧ

Tosser   Ⓣ

Player   ◯

Player
New Position   ◌

Path of Player ⟶

Ball Cart   ▢

Explanation: The first player blocks in the left front (#4) position. After blocking, player 1 turns and plays a tossed ball back to the coach. The player then runs to the left back (#5) position, assumes ready position, and digs two hard-driven spikes from a tosser. Next, player 1 runs to the right back (#1) position, where a second tosser tosses a ball so that player 1 has to dive to play the ball. (At this time, the second player starts at station #1.) The first player now moves to the right front (#2) position to hit a high ball tossed by the coach. After hitting, player 1 moves to the center and hits a "2" ball. As player 1 finishes with the attack, player 1 blocks player 2's regular hit in position #2 and then blocks the "2" ball from the center front (#3) position.

Setter's Drill

Contributor: Jodi Manore
University of Toledo

Purpose: To train setters how to penetrate to the net and set, cover the spiker, and return to defensive position. Also works spiker training against the block and blocker training.

Key:

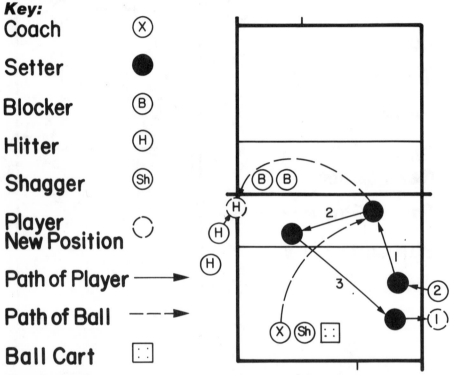

Coach	(X)
Setter	●
Blocker	(B)
Hitter	(H)
Shagger	(Sh)
Player New Position	◯
Path of Player	⟶
Path of Ball	⇢
Ball Cart	⬚

Explanation: The coach tosses to the setter's position at the net. The setter must penetrate to the net and set the ball to the left front (#4) position, where a spiker hits against a two-player block. The setter must cover the spiker, then return to defensive position in the right back (#1) position. As soon as the attacker has spiked the ball, the coach tosses a second ball for the next setter to penetrate and set to a second hitter. Continue the drill 10-15 times.

Variations:
1. Add diggers.
2. Vary the type of set.
3. Vary the position of the tosser.

Transition and Attack Four-to-One Drill

Contributor: Ralph Hippolyte
French National Volleyball Team

Purpose: To train dig recovery, dropping off the net, and line spiking.

Key:

Coach on Table ⊠

Blocker Ⓑ

Digger Ⓓ

Hitter Ⓗ

Shagger Ⓢⓗ

Player
New Position ◠

Path of Player ——→

Path of Ball – – →

Ball Cart ⊡

Setter/Target ●

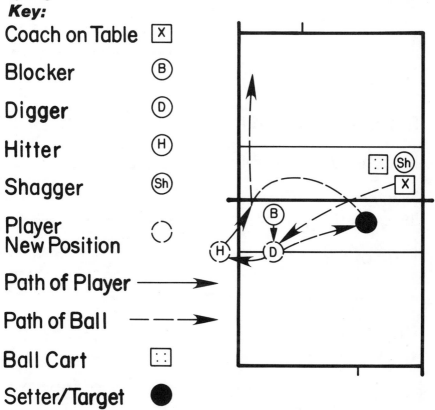

Explanation: The coach tosses to the setter's position at the net. The setter must penetrate to the net and set the ball to the left front (#4) position, where a spiker hits against a two-player block. The setter must cover the spiker, then return to defensive position in the right back (#1) position. As soon as the attacker has spiked the ball, the coach tosses a second ball for the next setter to penetrate and set to a second hitter. Continue the drill 10-15 times.

Variations:
1. Add diggers.
2. Vary the type of set.
3. Vary the position of the tosser.

Quick Attack Drill

Contributor: Ralph Hippolyte
French National Volleyball Team

Purpose: To train setting and two-player combinations.

Key:

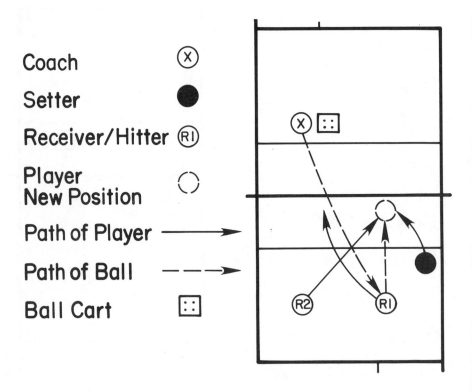

Coach   ⓧ

Setter   ●

Receiver/Hitter   ⓡ

Player
New Position   ◯

Path of Player   ⟶

Path of Ball   - - ⟶

Ball Cart   ⊡

Explanation: The coach throws or serves to either receiver. The setter penetrates and sets a specific combination depending on who passed the ball. If R1 passes, R2 goes for a quick and R1 goes for a middle set 3-5 feet above the net in front of the setter. If R2 passes, R1 goes for a half shoot and R2 goes for a middle set 3-5 feet above the net. Continue the drill for a specific time limit or a specific number of successful executions.

Block Two Drill

Contributor: Ralph Hippolyte
French National Volleyball Team

Purpose: To train double block, communication, and movement.

Key:

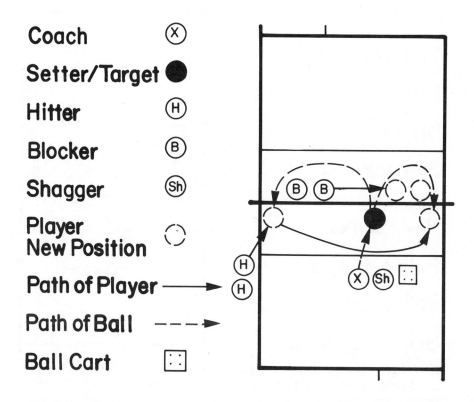

Coach	Ⓧ
Setter/Target	●
Hitter	Ⓗ
Blocker	Ⓑ
Shagger	(Sh)
Player New Position	⟲
Path of Player	⟶
Path of Ball	⇢
Ball Cart	⊡

Explanation: The coach tosses a ball to the setter, who sets a high ball to the left front (#4) position. The first hitter tries to spike through or around the two opposing blockers. Immediately after the spike, the coach tosses another ball to the setter, who sets to the right front (#2) position. The first hitter sprints to position #2 to spike the second set. The blockers quickly move into position to try to block the spike. Repeat the same sequence with a new hitter. Continue for a set time limit or a specific number of successful blocks.

Three Trips Drill

Contributor: Vivian Frausto
Indiana State University

Purpose: To practice setting and hitting different positions; to work on blocking in specialty positions.

Key:

Coach	Ⓧ
Setter/Target	●
Hitter	Ⓗ
Blocker	Ⓑ
Shagger	ⓢₕ
Player New Position	⃝
Path of Player	⟶
Path of Ball	- - -➤
Ball Cart	⊡

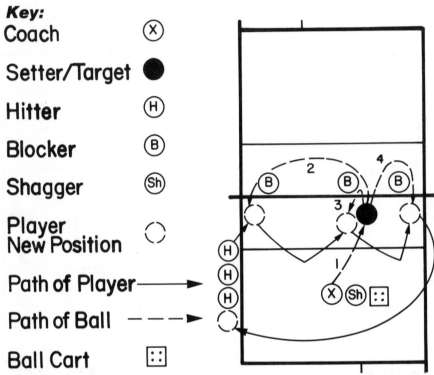

Explanation: The coach tosses to the setter, who sets the first ball to the left front (#4) position, the second to the center front (#3) position, and the third to the right front (#2) position. The hitter spikes from position #4, backs off, and approaches for a quick set in the middle, then backs off and approaches for a spike from position #2. The hitter then returns to the end of the hitting line. Blockers either block or back up to play defense, depending on the position of the hitter. After each hitter had gone through the sequence three times, groups rotate.

Variations:
1. Set to any of the three areas used in plays.
2. Add diggers.

Endurance Hitting and Blocking Drill

Contributor: Bob Gambardella
United States Military Academy

Purpose: To work on quick transition from blocking to attack, and to develop endurance.

Key:

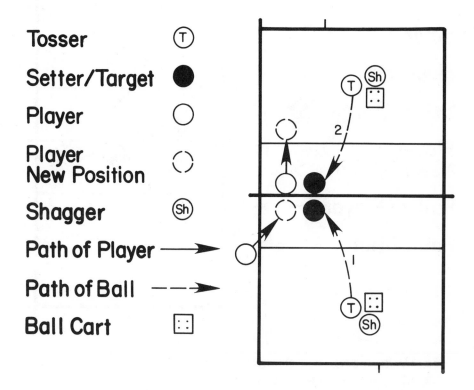

Tosser	(T)
Setter/Target	●
Player	○
Player New Position	(○)
Shagger	(Sh)
Path of Player	⟶
Path of Ball	--⟶
Ball Cart	[::]

Explanation: Toss to the setter, who sets a hitter on the bottom court. The opposing setter and hitter try to block the spike. Immediately after the spike, the top-court tosser tosses to the setter, who sets a hitter. The bottom court setter and hitter try to block the spike. The drill continues for a specified time or until a team has blocked a certain number of balls.

Hit, Then Go Block Drill

Contributor: Cheryl Alexander
California State College

Purpose: To practice closing a block, spiking against a block, and physical conditioning.

Key:

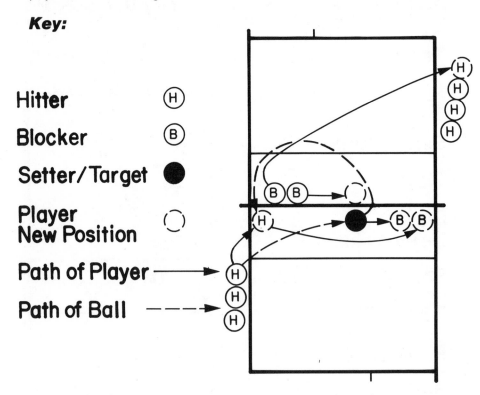

Hitter   (H)

Blocker   (B)

Setter/Target   ●

Player
New Position   ◯

Path of Player   ⟶

Path of Ball   --->

Explanation: The hitter tosses to the middle blocker, who sets to the hitter. The hitter tries to spike past the block, then goes to the right front (#2) position and becomes the outside blocker. This player and the middle blocker try to block a spike from the hitter opposite them. As soon as this play is complete, the next hitter in line tosses to the middle blocker, and the sequence continues. Players should shag the ball after blocking and rotate only on the same side.

Variation:
1. Decrease the number of players to increase the conditioning involved.

Three-Player-Technique Blocking Drill

Contributor: Mike Puritz
University of California-Irvine

Purpose: To work on blocking techniques during one-on-one situations and double blocks; to train the off blocker's movement from the net to defense position.

Key:

Hitter (H)

Blocker (B)

Shagger (Sh)

Chair ⊓

Path of Player ───────▶

Path of Ball ─ ─ ─ ─ ▶

Ball Cart ⊡

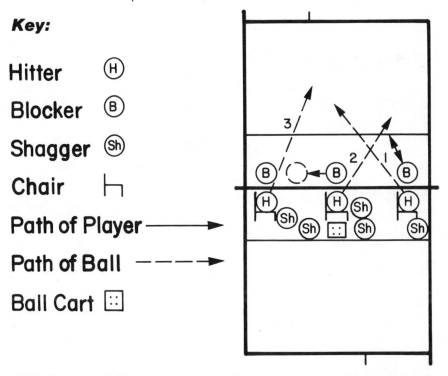

Explanation: The right front (#2) hitter spikes crosscourt, with the blocker opposite practicing one-on-one technique. The middle hitter spikes the power angle, with the middle blocker blocking one-on-one. The middle blocker uses correct footwork to join the position #2 blocker as the left front (#4) position hitter tries to hit past the block. During the third spike, the off blocker should come off the net for the sharp angle hit or dink. The same three steps are performed again, this time beginning with the position #4 hitter.

Variation:
1. Add defenders.

Dig, Dive, and Drive Drill

Contributor: Lynn Fielitz
University of Tennessee

Purpose: To practice digging and emergency techniques, playing balls out of the net, spiking transition, and conditioning.

Key:

Coach	Ⓧ
Digger	Ⓓ
Setter/Target	●
Player New Position	◯
Shagger	ⓢ
Path of Player	⟶
Path of Ball	⇢
Ball Cart	⊡

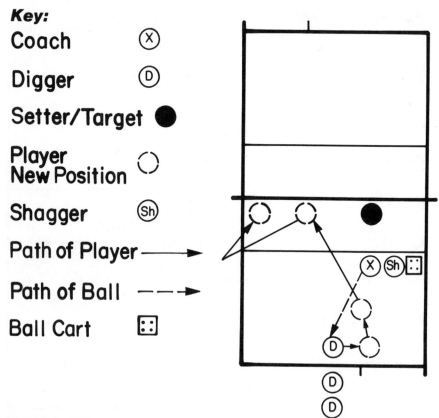

Explanation: The coach hits directly at the center back (#6) position for the player to dig; hits a ball to the right back (#1) position for a diving save; and then hits the ball in front of the player so a sprawl or dive must be used. The player then runs to the net and plays a ball out of the net on the same side of the court. Next the player backpedals and makes three attacks on sets coming from a setter. Work the drill with groups of threes, with each player going through three times and then becoming a shagger.

Variations:
1. Vary sets to the hitter.
2. Run the same drill using digs without dives.
3. Add a block.

Inside Out Drill

Contributor: Ralph Hippolyte
French National Volleyball Team

Purpose: To train mobility of spikers.

Key:

Coach	(X)
Receiver	(R)
Setter/Target	●
Hitter	(H)
Player New Position	◌
Shagger	(Sh)
Path of Player	——→
Path of Ball	- - -→
Ball Cart	⊡

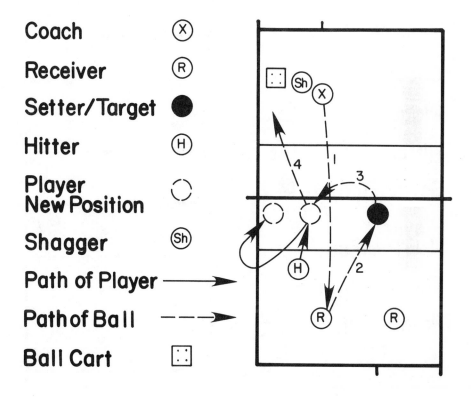

Explanation: The coach tosses a ball to the receiver in the left back (#5) position, who passes to the setter. The setter sets the hitter, who spikes a cut-back shot to position #2. Quickly, the coach tosses a second ball to the player in the right back (#1) position, who passes to the setter. The setter sets a high ball to the hitter, who must recover from the first attack, get outside, and hit deep crosscourt.

Partner Dig, Set, and Spike Drill
Contributor: Tina Bertucci
University of Tennessee

Purpose: To practice digging accuracy, setting, spiking, and teamwork.

Key:

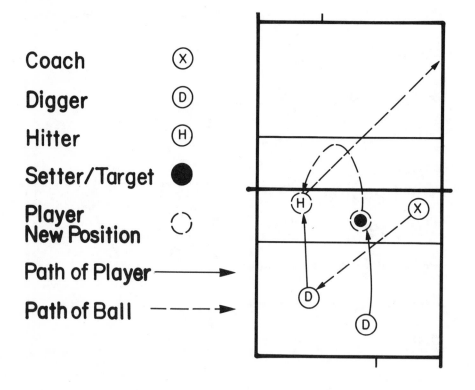

Coach   Ⓧ

Digger   Ⓓ

Hitter   Ⓗ

Setter/Target   ●

Player
New Position   ◌

Path of Player ⟶

Path of Ball ╌╌➤

Explanation: The coach spikes at either digger. The player who does not receive sets to the partner to spike. Both players quickly return to base positions and the drill continues for a specified goal or amount of time.

Two-Player Complex Training Drill

Contributor: Hiroshi Toyoda (Japan)
Director of Japanese Volleyball Association

Purpose: To master the combined skills of digging, setting, and spiking in actual game situations.

Key:

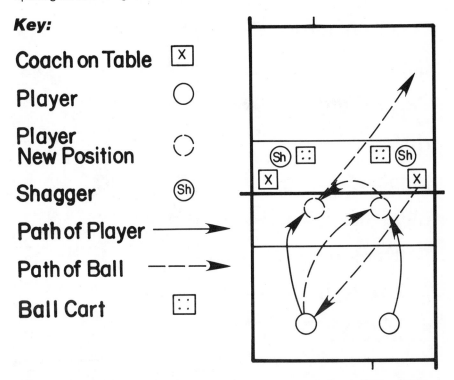

Coach on Table	X
Player	◯
Player New Position	◌
Shagger	Sh
Path of Player	⟶
Path of Ball	⤏
Ball Cart	⊡

Explanation: Two players start, one in the left back (#5) position and the other in the right back (#1) position. There are two coaches, located on the opposite side of the net in the right and left front (#2 and #4) positions. The coach in #4 position spikes to the player in #5 position. The player digs the ball and the partner in #1 position penetrates to set the ball. The ball is set to the player from #5 position for a spike. Then the sequence is repeated from the other side.

Variations:
1. Coaches spike down the line and run the same drill.
2. Vary the height, speed, and position of the set.
3. The coaches act as blockers when the set is positioned outside.

Transition Quick Attack Drill

Contributor: Mike Wilton
Cal Poly San Luis Obispo

Purpose: To work transition from blocking to quick attack.

Key:

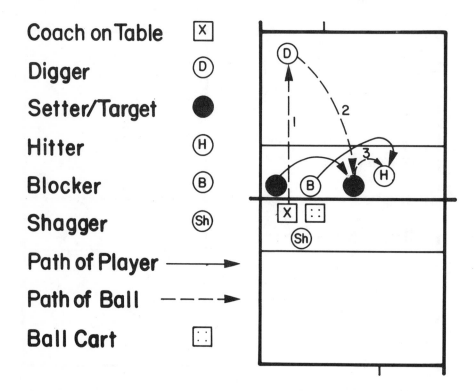

Coach on Table   ⊠

Digger   Ⓓ

Setter/Target   ●

Hitter   Ⓗ

Blocker   Ⓑ

Shagger   ⓢʰ

Path of Player   ——————▶

Path of Ball   – – – –▶

Ball Cart   ⊡

Explanation: The coach hits at a digger, while a quick hitter and the setter block jump. The hitter and setter turn low in the direction of the ball and the hitter backs off the net. The setter sets quick (shoot or one-set) to the hitter. Make the drill goal-oriented for the hitter, e.g., 10 balls down.

Variations:
1. Move the digger to the left back (#5) position.
2. Move the coach to the right front or middle front position.
3. Add a blocker for more of a challenge.

Deep Set Volley Drill

Contributor: Barbara L. Viera and Paul Damico
University of Delaware

Purpose: To learn to attack the opponent's position #1 on a broken play.

Key:

Coach	(X)
Digger	(D)
Setter	●
Hitter	(H)
Shagger	(Sh)
Player New Position	◯
Path of Player	⟶
Path of Ball	----⟶
Ball Cart	⊡

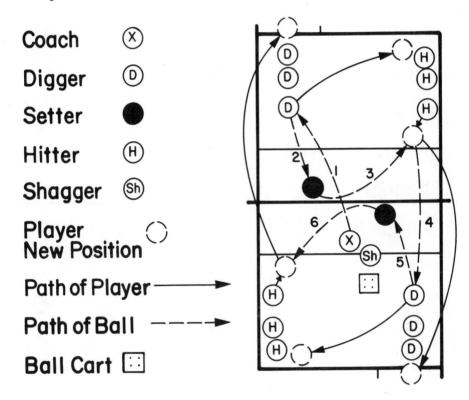

Explanation: The coach begins the drill by tossing to the right back (#1) position on either side. That player passes to the setter. The setter sets to the attack line or deeper. The hitter spikes the ball toward position #1 of the opponent's court. The digger plays the ball to the setter and the drill continues. Set a goal for a specific number of volleys without a miss.

Three-on-Three Exchange Drill

Contributor: Dave Olbright
University of Houston

Purpose: To practice overall team play in threes; to train deep-court hitting.

Key:

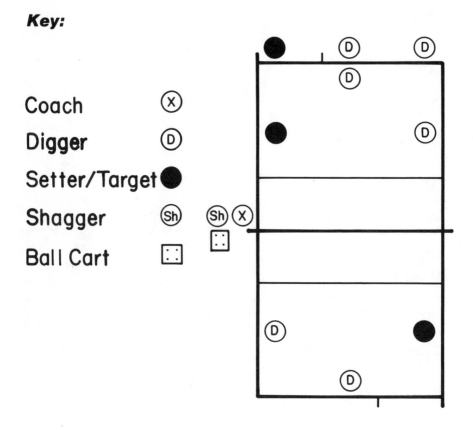

Coach — (X)

Digger — (D)

Setter/Target — ●

Shagger — (Sh)

Ball Cart — ⊡

Explanation: The teams volley back and forth, using deep-court hits. When an error stops the volley, the coach duplicates the ball that caused the error to the player who committed it. After each third hit by the coach, three new players assume defense position. Players should try for 15 consecutive volleys.

Defense-to-Offense Conversion Drill

Contributor: Pat Sullivan
George Washington University

Purpose: To practice reading skills and an accurate dig to the setter; to allow the setter to make a good offensive play from a dig.

Key:

Coach	(X)
Setter/Target	●
Hitter	(H)
Digger	(D)
Shagger	(Sh)
Player New Position	◯ (dashed)
Path of Player	——▶
Path of Ball	---▶
Ball Cart	⊡

Explanation: The coach tosses to the setter, who sets to any of the three hitters. The hitter spikes and the defense on the opposite side tries to counterattack with a dig to the setter and a spike by the hitter in the left front (#4) position. Substitute four new players after the defense has successfully run 10 counterattacks.

Variations:
1. Run combination sets to the hitters.
2. Have the setter try to block the counterattack.

Team Pepper Drill

Contributor: Mike Puritz
University of California-Irvine

Purpose: To work on defensive positioning, team communication, team ball control, and conditioning.

Key:

Setter/Target ●

Blocker Ⓑ

Hitter Ⓗ

Digger Ⓓ

Player
New Position ○

Path of Player ——→

Path of Ball – – –→

Explanation: The center front sets a high ball to either the right front or left front hitter. The ball is spiked with control at one of the defenders. Balls are dug to the center front, who sets to either the left front or right front hitter. Run the drill for two minutes before players rotate positions.

Variation:
1. All players can play all positions, or they can play their specialized positions for three rotations.

4

FOUR-SKILL DRILLS

Serve-and-Dig Drill

Contributor: Tina Bertucci
University of Tennessee

Purpose: To train the serve and dig sequence, serving, serve receive, and spiking.

Key:

Server   ⓢ

Receiver   ⓡ

Setter/Target   ●

Hitter   Ⓗ

Player
New Position   ◌

Path of Player ⟶

Path of Ball --➤

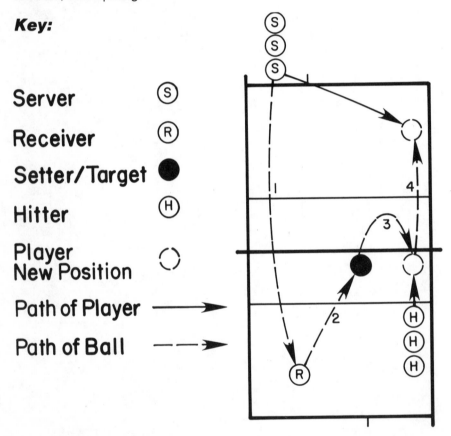

Explanation: The first server serves to the receiver, then moves to the left back (#5) position. The receiver passes to the setter, who backsets to a spiker in the right front (#2) position. The spiker hits down the line to the server. If the receiver's pass is not accurate, the coach tosses a ball to the setter to keep the drill going.

Variations
1. Have the server play different defense positions.
2. Vary the position of the receiver or spiker.

Save-the-Setter Drill

Contributor: Mike English
University of Missouri

Purpose: To work on ball control and to run the offense off the transition from defense to offense.

Key:

Coach on Table $\boxed{\text{x}}$

Blocker   Ⓑ

Hitter   Ⓗ

Setter/Target ●

Digger   Ⓓ

Shagger   (Sh)

Player
New Position   ◯

Chair   ⊓

Path of Player ———▶

Ball Cart $\boxed{::}$

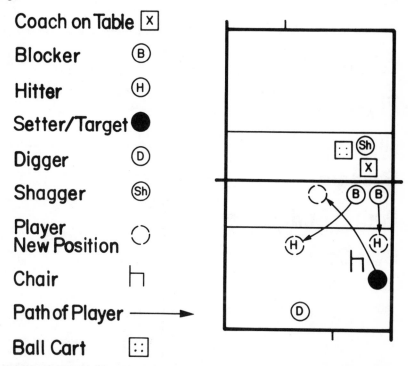

Explanation: The coach stands on a table and hits past the blockers at a digger. The setter penetrates from behind a chair in the right back (#1) position and sets a designated play for the right front blocker and middle blocker. Immediately after a successful counter-attack, two new players replace the blockers-hitters and the second setter is in position to repeat the drill.

Variations:
1. Spike the ball to the setter, forcing the right front player to set.
2. Run the drill from the opposite side or middle.
3. Add another digger and spike at the seam between them.
4. Vary the offense run on the counterattack.

Boo-Boo Drill

Contributor: Judith Novinc
James Madison University

Purpose: To work on communication, court coverage, and conditioning.

Key:

Coach	Ⓧ
Player	◯
Digger	Ⓓ
Shagger	(Sh)
Path of Ball	- - - ➤
Ball Cart	⊡

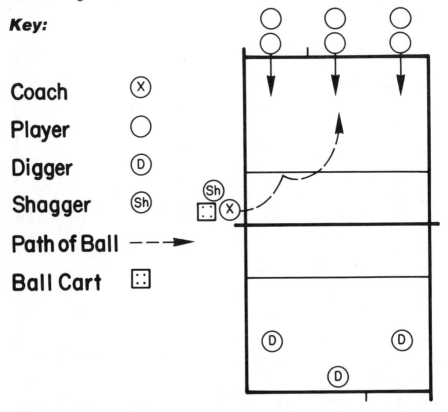

Explanation: The coach spikes the ball against the floor. The players behind the endline run in, call the ball, and play out the volley against the opposing defense. Winners stay on as the new defensive team and losers go to the sideline to do any combination of conditioning activities (e.g. pushups, situps, tuck jumps) before going to the end of the line.

Variations:

1. Players start by lying face down on the endline.
2. Players start at the net, facing the net. The coach spikes the ball behind them, and they turn around to play the ball.

Deep-Tip Combination Drill

Contributor: Niels Pedersen
2nd City Limited Volleyball Club

Purpose: To work ball control in serving, passing, setting, and tipping; teamwork.

Key:

Server	(S)
Receiver	(R)
Setter/Target	●
Hitter	(H)
Shagger	(Sh)
Player New Position	◌
Path of Player	⟶
Path of Ball	⇢
Ball Cart	⊡

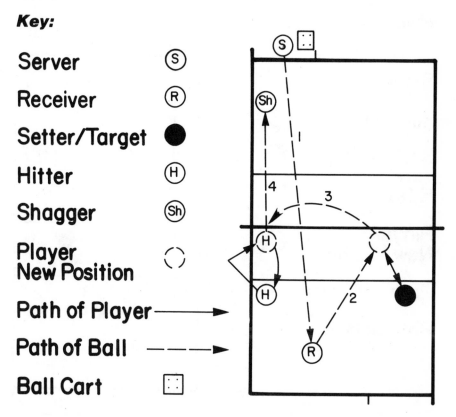

Explanation: The server serves to a receiver in the left back (#5) position. The receiver passes to a penetrating setter, who sets to the left front (#4) position. The hitter tips to the opponent's position #1. The drill is repeated until a prescribed number of successful executions are completed. Rotate clockwise.

Variations:
1. Tip crosscourt.
2. Add blockers.
3. Add more players in each position.

Pass, Set, and Hit Drill

Contributor: Dave Olbright
University of Houston

Purpose: To work on communication during serve receive and to practice spiking down the line.

Key:

Server Ⓢs

Receiver Ⓡr

Setter/Target ●

Hitter Ⓗh

Player New Position ⌒⌒

Path of Player ───▶

Path of Ball ──--▶

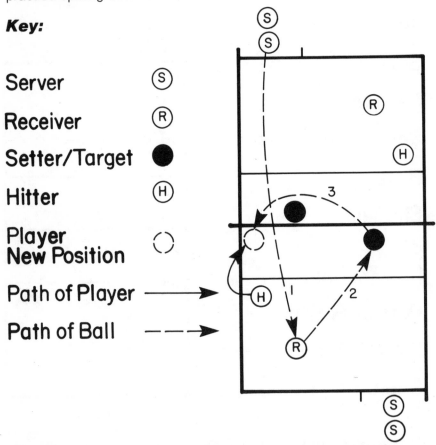

Explanation: The server serves between the two receivers. The ball is passed to the setter, who sets to the left front (#4) position. The hitter approaches and spikes down the line. After 10 good spikes, players rotate positions. Run the drill on both sides, alternating serves.

Variations:
1. Have the setter attempt to block the spike.
2. Vary the positions of the hitter and receiver.

Beat-the-Ball Drill

Contributor: Ginger Mayson
Kansas State University

Purpose: Concentration and pinpoint accuracy on serve, receive, set, and spike.

Key:

Server	S
Receiver	R
Setter/Target	●
Player New Position	◌
Hitter	H
Path of Player	——→
Path of Ball	---→

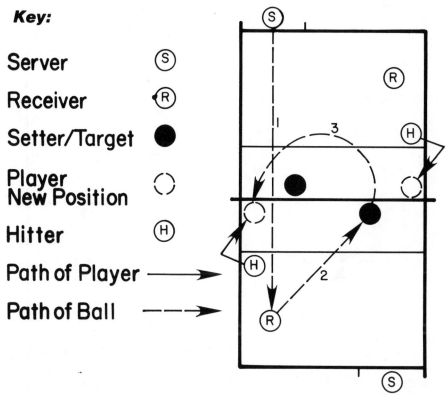

Explanation: Players must direct serves, passes, sets, and hits to a section of the court designated by the coach. Balls are served by both sides at the same time, directly to the receivers. The pass must go to the setter without any movement of the setter's feet and the hit must be directed back to the server with the server taking no more than two steps to retrieve the hit. Each successful execution earns 1 point. The ball starts out with 10 points and the players must reach 15 before the ball. If the ball wins the players on the losing side(s) must do the designated "punishment."

Variation:
1. Change players' position on the court.

Serve with Two-Player Receive-and-Attack Drill

Contributor: Vivian Frausto
Indiana State University

Purpose: To develop serve placement, passing to a target area, backing up, and communication.

Key:

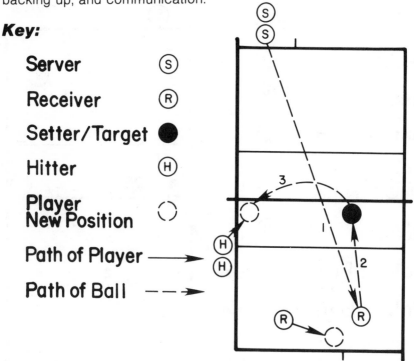

Server	Ⓢ
Receiver	Ⓡ
Setter/Target	●
Hitter	Ⓗ
Player New Position	◌
Path of Player	——→
Path of Ball	– –→

Explanation: The first server serves to the receiver in the right back (#1) position. This receiver calls for the ball and passes to the setter. The other receiver backs up the play. The setter sets to the hitter in the left front (#4) position who approaches, jumps, and catches or spikes the ball to the server. The second server serves to the receiver in the left back (#5) position and the sequence is repeated. Rotate from servers to receivers to setter to spikers after five good passes.

Variations:
1. The coach calls crosscourt or line serves.
2. The spiker moves to middle or right front position.
3. Add blockers and diggers into the rotation.

Three-Player Serve-Receive and Attack Drill

Contributor: Stephanie Schleuder
University of Minnesota

Purpose: To concentrate and perfect team serve receive fundamentals while giving all players the opportunity to pass, set, hit, and serve.

Key:

Server	Ⓢ
Receiver	Ⓡ
Setter/Target	●
Player New Position	◌
Shagger	Ⓢⁿ
Path of Player	→
Path of Ball	--→
Ball Cart	⊡

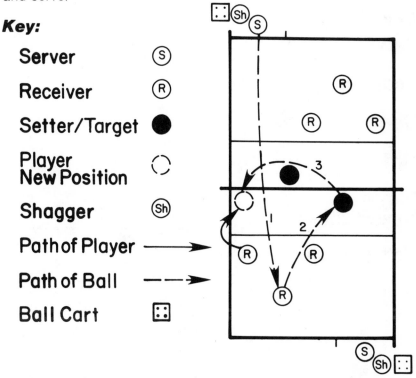

Explanation: Divide the team into groups of five players. On each side of the net one player serves, one sets, and three receive, using only half of the court. The receivers must successfully pass 10 balls to the setter, who then sets to either front-row player for a hit. After 10 successful passes, sets, and hits, the players rotate to new positions.

Variations:
1. Run the same drill without the setting and hitting if more concentration on passing is desired.
2. Vary the position of the receivers.

Serve-to-Three-and-Attack Drill

Contributor: Kay Woodiel
Arkansas State University

Purpose: To work on serve reception, setting, service placement, and spiking.

Key:

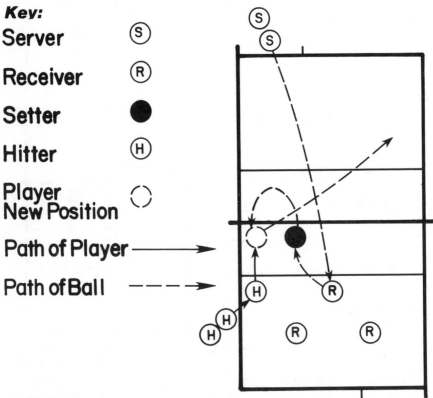

Server	Ⓢ
Receiver	Ⓡ
Setter	●
Hitter	Ⓗ
Player New Position	◌
Path of Player	⟶
Path of Ball	---→

Explanation: Three receivers line up in a triangle, simulating the three center players of a W formation. Each server must serve six balls, two to each position. Receivers attempt to pass to a setter positioned at the net. The setter sets to hitters in the right front (#2) position. After each group completes its turn, the players rotate.

Variations:
1. Vary the receivers' position.
2. Vary the position of the attackers.
3. Have the server assume defense position.

One-on-One Serve-Receive Drill

Contributor: Jan Yandell
Former Head Volleyball Coach, Idaho State University

Purpose: To develop serving and passing accuracy; to practice spiking from the right front (#2) position.

Key:

Server	Ⓢ
Receiver	Ⓡ
Setter/Target	●
Hitter	Ⓗ
Player New Position	◌
Path of Player	→
Path of Ball	→

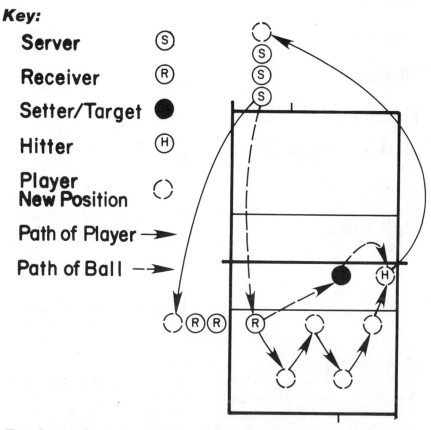

Explanation: The first server serves five balls, one to each receiving position. As soon as the receiver passes to the setter, the next ball is served. The setter backsets to the receiver in the right front (#2) position. After spiking, the player goes to the end of the serving line. The other receivers quickly move to the next receiving position. After serving, the server moves to the receiving line.

Variation:
1. Have the spiker become a blocker before going to serve.

Signal-the-Setter Drill

Contributor: Ralph Hippolyte
French National Volleyball Team

Purpose: To train peripheral vision and quick thinking.

Key:

Coach   (X)

Server   (S)

Hitter   (H)

Receiver   (R)

Setter/Target ●

Shagger   (Sh)

Ball Cart   [∴]

Explanation: A player throws or serves to the receiver, who passes to the setter penetrating to the net. As the ball is descending toward the setter, the coach on the other side of the net signals the setter with one of three flags. Depending on which flag is shown, the setter must decide what and where to set. For example, a yellow flag means short behind to the hitter in the right front (#2) position; a green flag means short in front to the hitter in the middle front (#3) position; and a red flag means half-shoot to the player in the left front (#4) position.

Variation:
1. Vary the play sets designated by the flags.

Combination-Play Decision Drill

Contributor: Lynn Fielitz
University of Tennessee

Purpose: To teach players to quickly decide which combination play to run depending on who receives the serve.

Key:

Server	(S)
Receiver	(R)
Hitter	(H)
Setter	●
Player New Position	○
Path of Player	——→
Path of Ball	---→

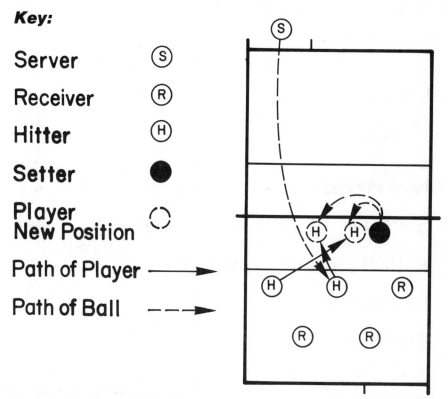

Explanation: Players set up in W serve-reception formation. The setter selects one of two plays involving the left front (#4) position player and the middle front (#3) position player. If the #3 position player receives the serve, then run a play requiring the #4 position player to move first (e.g., #4 to spike in #3 and #3 goes to #4). If anyone other than the player in #3 position receives the serve, the player in #3 moves first.

Variations:
1. Have the setter use different play sets, requiring the nonpassing player in the front row to run the faster pattern.
2. Use three front-row players.
3. Add spiker coverage.

Four-Skill Movement Drill

Contributor: Ralph Hippolyte
French National Volleyball Team

Purpose: To train player movement sequence in four skills.

Key:

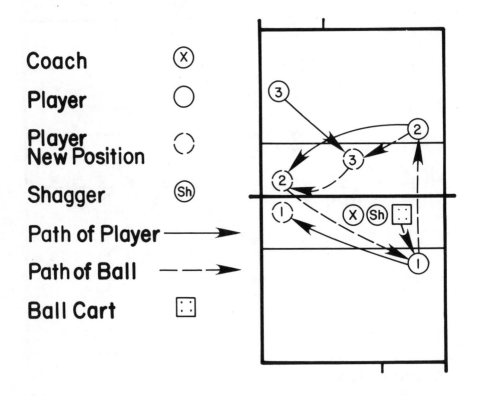

Coach   Ⓧ

Player   ◯

Player New Position   ⌒⌄

Shagger   ⒮ⓗ

Path of Player ⟶

Path of Ball ⟶

Ball Cart   ⊡

Explanation: The coach tosses a ball to player 1, who sets over the net to player 2. Player 2 passes to player 3, who has moved to position #3. Player 3 then sets a backset to position #2, where player 2 has already moved in order to spike against player 1's block into the opponent's position #2. Return to base positions.

Endurance Blocking Drill

Contributor: Janice Hudson
Texas Tech University

Purpose: To work on individual blocking skills and positioning; endurance.

Key:

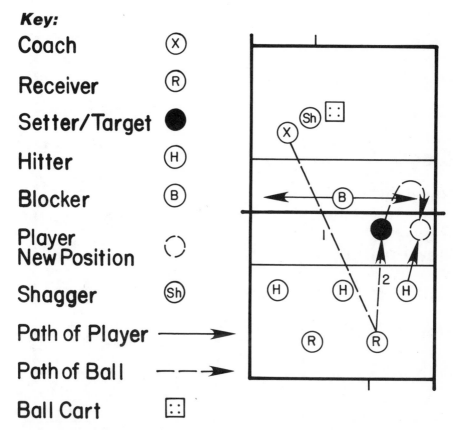

Coach   Ⓧ

Receiver   Ⓡ

Setter/Target   ⬤

Hitter   Ⓗ

Blocker   Ⓑ

Player
New Position   ◌

Shagger   ⓢʰ

Path of Player   ⟶

Path of Ball   ⇢

Ball Cart   ⊡

Explanation: The coach serves to one of the receivers. The receiver passes to the setter. The setter sets any of the three hitters. The blocker must react to the set and move to block. As soon as the hitter has landed, the next pass has already been made to the setter, so the drill moves rapidly. After the blocker blocks 10 balls, a shagger becomes the new blocker. The hitters rotate one position to the right, and another shagger becomes a hitter.

Variation:
1. Have two blockers working together.

Variation Drill

Contributor: Carolyn Condit
Xavier University

Purpose: To work on setting from the backcourt, spiking a set from this angle, and digging when no block has formed.

Key:

Coach	(X)
Receiver	(R)
Hitter	(H)
Digger	(D)
Shagger	(Sh)
Player New Position	◯
Path of Player	──────▶
Path of Ball	── ── ──▶
Ball Cart	⬚

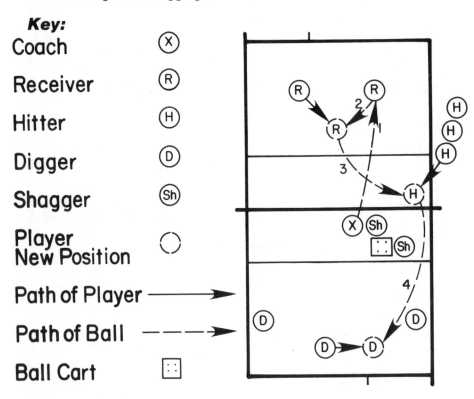

Explanation: The coach tosses to either receiver, who passes the ball high toward the other receiver. This receiver sets to the hitter in the left front (#4) position. The three diggers work to pass the ball spiked by the hitter. Players can stay at the same station for several rounds, or they can rotate to a new area after each attack.

Variations:
1. Run the same drill using a weak-side attack.
2. Add blockers.
3. Have one of the players on defense put a free ball over the net to initiate the drill.

Three-Three-Three Drill

Contributor: Niels Pedersen
2nd City Limited Volleyball Club

Purpose: Varies depending on the needs of the team. Areas of emphasis can be: team blocking, serve reception, attack combinations, freeball execution, and spiker coverage.

Key:

Coach	(X)
Hitter	(H)
Receiver	(R)
Blocker	(B)
Setter/Target	●
Shagger	(Sh)
Ball Cart	[::]

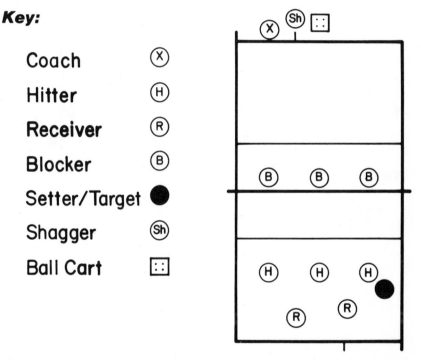

Explanation: Divide the team into three groups of three, each group consisting of a setter/offsetter, outside hitter, and middle blocker. One group blocks, one group attacks, one group passes. The coach serves to the passing group, who passes to the setter. The setter sets to one of the three attackers, while the blocking group tries to stop the hitter. Set a goal of 10 balls to be successfully blocked, spiked, or passed, depending on the area of concentration.

Variations:
1. Vary the coach's position and type of serve or toss.
2. Use different attack combinations.
3. Vary serve reception patterns.
4. Add a serving group.

Monster "D" Drill

Contributor: Bob Bertucci
University of Tennessee

Purpose: To develop full-service reception and attack, attack serve, and individual defense.

Key:

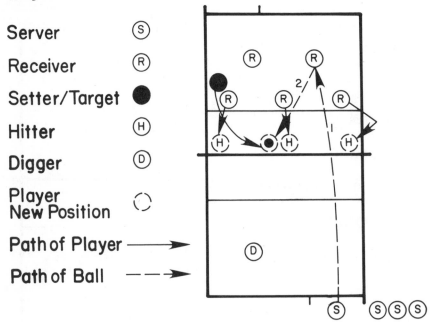

Server	(S)
Receiver	(R)
Setter/Target	●
Hitter	(H)
Digger	(D)
Player New Position	(⌐)
Path of Player	⟶
Path of Ball	---⟶

Explanation: One side lines up in their usual service reception formation. They will pass serve and attack, using all their play sequences. The servers will be instructed to serve every ball for an ace. The server receives 2 points for each ace and loses 1 point for an error. There is only one digger, who is called the "monster." Every time the digger touches the ball, 1 point is awarded, 2 points are awarded for playing the ball up, and 3 points for a ball above the level of the net inside the attack line. The side that gets to 15 first is the winning team.

Variation:
1. Change players' positions on the court and require attackers to spike in a specific direction.

One-Hitter Spike-Block Drill

Contributor: Kizzie Mailander
West Chester State College

Purpose: To work on outside and middle hitting, and outside and middle blocking.

Key:

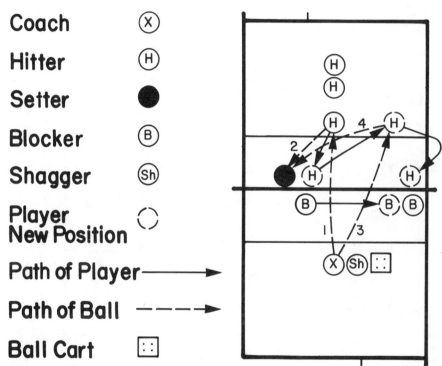

Coach	Ⓧ
Hitter	Ⓗ
Setter	●
Blocker	Ⓑ
Shagger	Ⓢⓗ
Player New Position	◯
Path of Player	—————▶
Path of Ball	– – – ▶
Ball Cart	⊡

Explanation: The coach tosses a ball to H. H passes to the setter and drives for a middle hit. The blocker on the opposite side tries to stop the spike. H then backpedals diagonally, receives another ball tossed from the coach, and passes to the setter. The setter sets high outside to H. The middle blocker joins the outside blocker and they try to block. Hitters and blockers rotate within their respective lines until the coach instructs them to switch sides of the net.

Variations:
1. The coach can be anyplace at the net.
2. Instead of shagging the set balls, set back to the coach and continue the drill.

Individual Drill

Contributor: Jan Yandell
Former Head Volleyball Coach,
Idaho State University

Purpose: To quickly have players use all situations found in volleyball.

Key:

Coach	Ⓧ
Player	◯
Player New Position	◌
Shagger	Ⓢⁿ
Path of Player	——▶
Path of Ball	---▶
Ball Cart	⊡

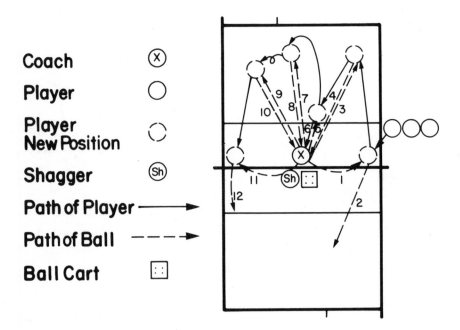

Explanation: The coach tosses the first ball for a spike. The player hits and backpedals to the left back (#5) position to pass. The coach tips one short, and the player must run and dive. Next the coach tosses high and deep. The player must get up quickly and set to the coach, who spikes so that the player must roll for the ball. Then the coach tosses a ball to the right front (#2) position for the player to tip. Each player should execute the sequence three times.

Variation:
1. Use different skills or combinations such as net recovery, serving, blocking, etc.

Box Coverage Drill

Contributor: Pat Sullivan
George Washington University

Purpose: To concentrate on watching your hitter and the opposition's block on coverage; to go for a blocked ball; to convert a blocked ball into a strong offensive play.

Key:

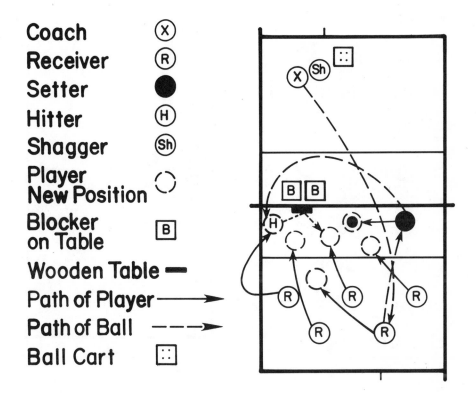

Coach	Ⓧ
Receiver	Ⓡ
Setter	●
Hitter	Ⓗ
Shagger	Ⓢⓗ
Player New Position	◌
Blocker on Table	B
Wooden Table	—
Path of Player	⟶
Path of Ball	---⟶
Ball Cart	⊡

Explanation: The coach serves or tosses a ball to the receiving team. The receiving team passes, sets, and hits into the block (a player on a table or chair holding a large box). Spiker coverage passes the ball and converts to an attack, which is blocked again. Try to keep the sequence going as long as possible.

Block-and-Recover Drill

Contributor: Ralph Hippolyte
French National Volleyball Team

Purpose: To train the middle blocker in movement patterns and mechanics of blocking.

Key:

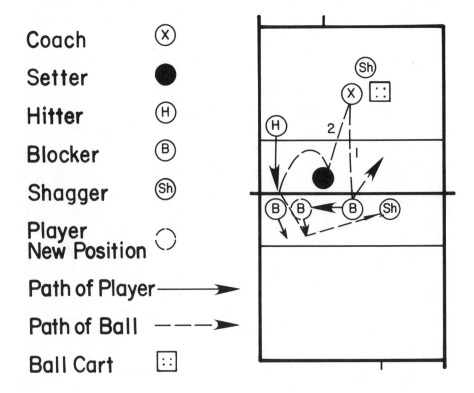

Coach	(X)
Setter	●
Hitter	(H)
Blocker	(B)
Shagger	(Sh)
Player New Position	(dashed circle)
Path of Player	⟶
Path of Ball	-- -⟶
Ball Cart	⊡

Explanation: The coach tosses a ball over the net for the blocker in the middle front (#3) position to block. The coach quickly tosses another ball to the setter, who sets a high ball to the hitter in the right front (#2) position. The middle blocker and a blocker in the left front (#4) position try to block. The hitter tips over and 3′ behind the middle blocker, who must play the ball up to a target.

Controlled Circuit Drill

Contributor: Arlene Ignico
Former Head Volleyball Coach, Austin Peay University

Purpose: To improve block recovery skill, digging, emergency techniques, and spiking.

Key:

Coach   (X)

Digger   (D)

Hitter   (H)

Blocker   (B)

Tosser   (T)

Shagger   (Sh)

Player
New Position   ○

Path of Player   ⟶

Path of Ball   ----►

Ball Cart   ⊡

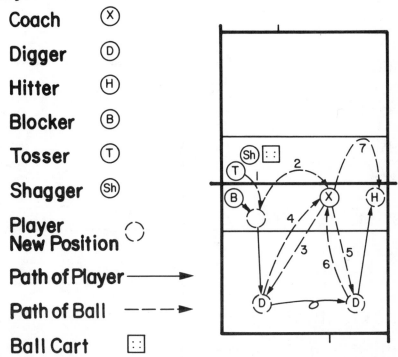

Explanation: The player begins the drill by mock blocking. On descent, a tosser throws the ball directly over and behind the blocker. This player must recover from the block, step, and pass the ball to the coach. The player immediately moves to set the same ball being passed by the coach to the left back (#5) position. The player digs this ball back to the coach, who quickly spikes again to the right back (#1) position. The player is still required to play the ball up so that the coach can set the ball to the right front (#2) position where the player finishes the circuit with a spike. This drill should require each player to make three successful trips through the circuit.

Variations:
1. Run the drill from the other side of the net.
2. The coach can decrease the intensity by self-setting between each station.

Transition and Attack Four-to-Four Drill

Contributor: Ralph Hippolyte
French National Volleyball Team

Purpose: To train spikers recovery and spiking from position #4 to #4.

Key:

Coach	Ⓧ
Blocker	Ⓑ
Digger	Ⓓ
Hitter	Ⓗ
Setter	●
Player New Position	◯
Path of Player	⟶
Path of Ball	--⟶
Ball Cart	⊡

Explanation: Set up an extra antenna, 5 feet inside the regulation antenna. The hitter starts at the net in the left front (#4) position, block jumps, and retreats into a deep middle front (#3) position. The coach tips to position #3 and the hitter plays the ball up to the setter. The hitter must immediately recover to position #4. The setter sets a high ball and the hitter must spike a sharp crosscourt angle inside the adjusted antenna.

Hitting and Team Defense Drill

Contributor: Linda J. Wambach
University of Evansville

Purpose: To work on team defense coordination, communication, and court coverage.

Key:

Coach	Ⓧ
Setter/Target	●
Blocker	Ⓑ
Hitter	◯
Digger	Ⓓ
Shagger	Ⓢ̲ʰ
Player New Position	◌
Path of Player	⟶
Path of Ball	- - -➤
Ball Cart	⊡

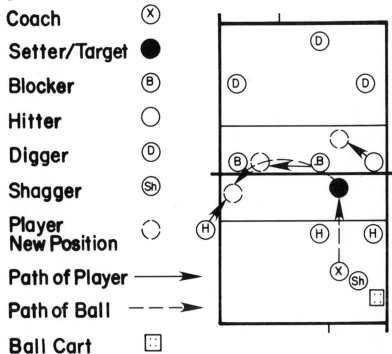

Explanation: The coach tosses a ball to the setter, who sets to one of three hitters. The defense reacts to the set and assumes defense positions. The defense plays the ball and makes transition to offense through to spiker coverage position. After 10 sets to each hitter, rotate so that hitters become blockers, blockers become backcourt defenders, defense becomes shaggers and setter, and shaggers and setter become hitters.

Variations:
1. Include offensive coverage on the hitting side.
2. Call plays for the hitting side.
3. Have hitters block the defense's counterattack.

Crosscourt Digging Transition Drill

Contributor: Jim Stone
Ohio State University

Purpose: To train crosscourt diggers on proper alignment inside the block; to work on transition from defense to offense.

Key:

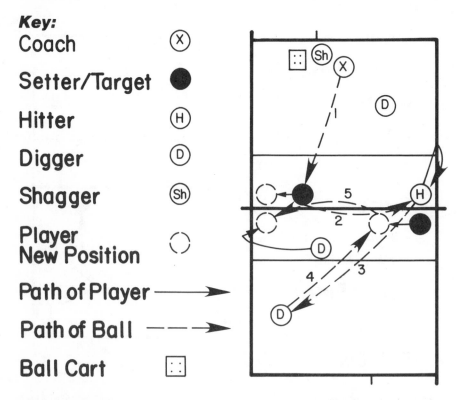

Coach   (X)

Setter/Target   ●

Hitter   (H)

Digger   (D)

Shagger   (Sh)

Player
New Position   ◯

Path of Player ⟶

Path of Ball - - ⟶

Ball Cart   ⊡

Explanation: The coach tosses to the setter/blocker. This player sets to the left front (#4) position, and the hitter tries to attack crosscourt. The players on the opposite side try to dig, set, and attack the players on the other side at a crosscourt angle. After setting, setters should block line, forcing hitters to go crosscourt. Priority is on accurate defense position of the left front and left back diggers, and accurate attacking by the hitters.

Variations:
1. Work on the setter coming from the back row to set.
2. Incorporate a center back into the drill.

5

FIVE-SKILL DRILLS

Server Transition Drill

Contributor: Ralph Hippolyte
French National Volleyball Team

Purpose: To train ball control and server's switch.

Key:

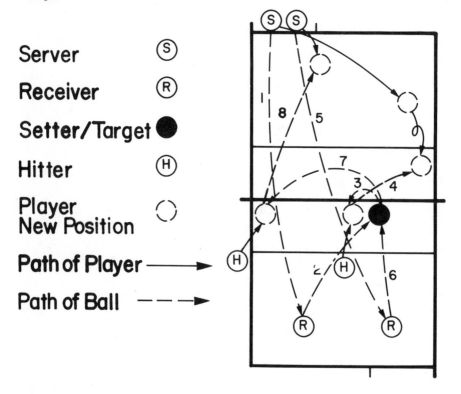

Server	ⓢ
Receiver	ⓡ
Setter/Target	●
Hitter	ⓗ
Player New Position	◯
Path of Player	——➤
Path of Ball	- - -➤

Explanation: The first server serves to the receiver in the left back (#5) position. After serving, the server sprints to play defense in position (#5). The receiver passes to the setter, who sets a quick ball to the hitter in the middle front (#3) position. The hitter tips the ball to the left front (#4) position and the server must play the ball to the target. The next server serves to the right back (#1) position. After serving, this server sprints to play defense in the middle back (#6) position. The receiver passes to the setter, who sets a high ball to a hitter in the #4 position. This hitter attacks deep middle, and the server must play the ball to the target. Continue the sequence with new servers.

Animal Drill

Contributor: Judith Novinc
James Madison University

Purpose: A multiskill drill used for conditioning.

Key:

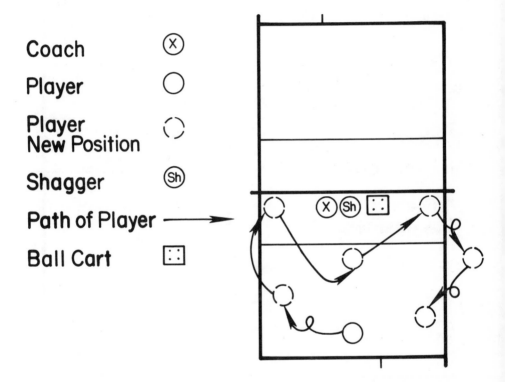

Coach (X)

Player ◯

Player New Position ◌

Shagger (Sh)

Path of Player ⟶

Ball Cart ⊡

Explanation: The first player goes through the following sequence: bump pass, roll for a ball, spike a toss, set a toss, mock block, roll left without a ball, roll right without a ball. The coach tosses balls for the first four contacts. Run the drill with groups of three, each player repeating the circuit three times.

Variation:
1. Increase the number of repetitions to increase the conditioning.

Loser's Pay Drill

Contributor: Ginger Mayson
Kansas State University

Purpose: Practice serve reception formations, passing accuracy, and play sets.

Key:

Server   Ⓢ

Receiver   Ⓡ

Hitter   Ⓗ

Blocker   Ⓑ

Setter/Target   ●

Player New Position   ◌

Path of Player ⟶

Path of Ball ⤑

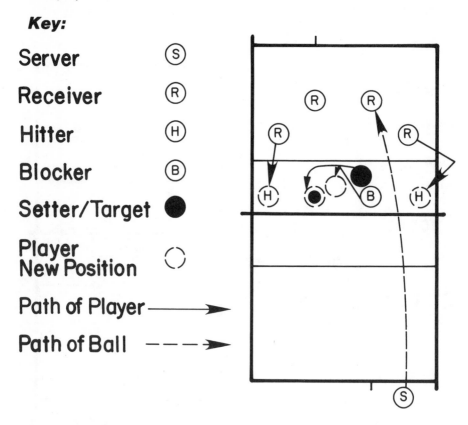

Explanation: Designate a serve reception formation and playset. The team must accurately execute pass and attack with no errors. The ball starts with 10 points and the team with 0. Each time the team passes and attacks successfully, the ball loses 1 point and the team gains 1 point. Play to 15 points. If the ball wins, players must perform exercises that are specified for the loser.

Variation:
1. Change loser's duties each day to fit the workout that the team is concentrating on for that day.

Multiple Offense Hitting-and-Blocking Drill

Contributor: Amanda Burk
University of Idaho

Purpose: To practice team attack and play sets from serve-receive positions; to work on blocking combinations.

Key:

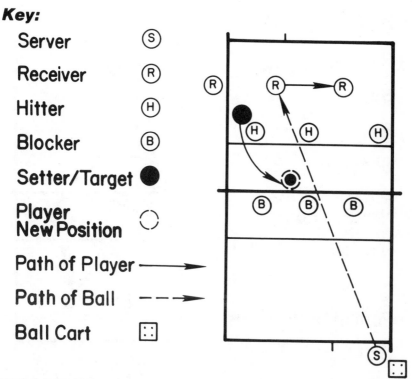

Server	(S)
Receiver	(R)
Hitter	(H)
Blocker	(B)
Setter/Target	●
Player New Position	○
Path of Player	—→
Path of Ball	- - →
Ball Cart	⊡

Explanation: The coach or a player alternates serving to the right back (#1) position and the left back (#5) position. The first receiver passes from position #1 and a play is run, then from position #5 and another play is run. Another receiver passes the next two serves and the receivers continue to alternate. Blockers should work together, reading and calling switches as the play demands. Continue the drill until a specific number of successful plays are executed.

Variation:

1. Have the setter penetrate from each of the three backcourt positions as well as the front court 5-1 positions.

Attack-and-Cover Drill

Contributor: Janice Hudson
Texas Tech University

Purpose: To practice pass, set, and spike sequence; to work on spiker coverage with resulting counterattack

Key:

Coach ⓧ

Receiver ⓡ

Setter ⬤

Hitter Ⓗ

Shagger ⓢⓗ

Player
New Position ⌒

Blocker on Table Ⓑ

Path of Player ⟶

Path of Ball ⇢

Ball Cart ⊡

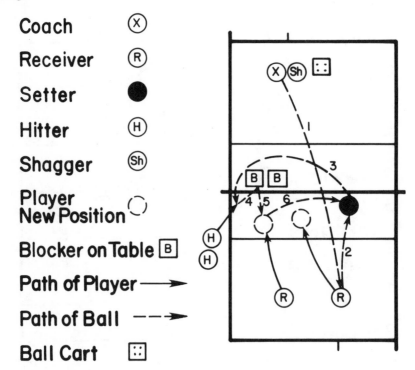

Explanation: The coach hits or tosses to the receivers, who pass to a setter in the target area, and the ball is set outside to the left front (#4) position. The hitters try to spike into blockers who are standing on tables. The ball is deflected into the hitter's court, and the attacking team covers and attempts a counterattack. After five times, rotate from blockers to shaggers, shaggers to passers, passers to hitters, and hitters to blockers.

Variation:
1. Use the setter as a participant in spiker coverage.

Three-Player Complex Training Drill

Contributor: Hiroshi Toyoda
Director of Japanese Volleyball Association

Purpose: To master the combination attack after service receptions, with spiker coverage and transition to blocking.

Key:

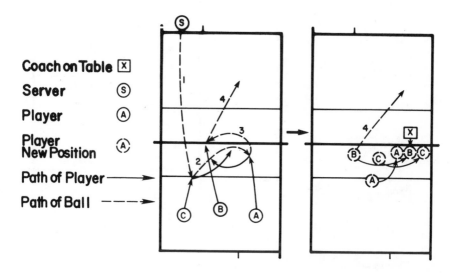

Coach on Table ☒

Server ⓢ

Player Ⓐ

Player New Position (Ⓐ)

Path of Player ⟶

Path of Ball ⟶

Explanation: Three players line up in the court for service reception and one server stands in the opponent's service area for service. The server serves to one of the three players. Another player should be the setter moving near the net. The two remaining players will be spikers after service reception. When one player spikes, the other two players move for spiker coverage. After the spike, all three players move to block in their positions near the net.

Trans-Combo Drill

Contributor: Debbie Sokol
Rice University

Purpose: To develop quick transition and movement patterns after executing a combination of skills.

Key:

Coach	Ⓧ
Server	Ⓢ
Receiver	Ⓡ
Setter	●
Blocker	Ⓑ
Shagger	Ⓢⱨ
Player New Position	◌
Path of Player	⟶
Path of Ball	‑‑‑➤
Ball Cart	⊡

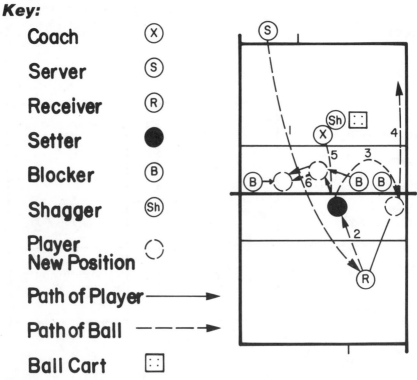

Explanation: The server serves to the receiver, who passes to the setter. The receiver now becomes a hitter and the ball is set and the hitter attacks against a two-player block. As the blockers descend, the coach tosses a ball into the net. The middle blocker retrieves the ball up to the right front player, who sets a fast attack to the middle players.

Variations:
1. Position the receiver in different spots on the court and have the attack at different positions at the net.
2. Have the coach toss the ball into the net so that the outside blockers have to play it off the block that stopped a middle attack.

Serve-Receive and Defense Doubles Drill

**Contributor: Mary Phyl Dwight
Former Head Volleyball Coach,
University of Iowa**

Purpose: To work on team serve reception; to challenge two players on defense.

Key:

Server	Ⓢ
Receiver	Ⓡ
Setter/Target	●
Hitter	Ⓗ
Digger	Ⓓ
Player	◯
Player New Position	◌
Path of Player	⟶
Path of Ball	⤍

Explanation: The group is divided into two teams—one receives while the other serves and plays defense. A player serves and joins a teammate on the court for defense. The pair receives 1 point if either player can play the ball after it has been spiked, tipped, etc. by the receiving team. The receiving team scores when the ball is played for a kill and is not touched by either defender. The receiving team should try to run the options off the serve receive they use in a game. The first team scoring 5 points wins, and the teams switch sides.

Variations:

1. Any ball touched by the defenders earns a point.
2. Use three defenders.
3. Allow the defenders to counterattack so that the receiving team works on transition.

Defensive Carousel

Contributor: Frank Fristensky
Eastern Michigan University

Purpose: To develop defense, serve, serve receive, setting, and hitting skills.

Key:

Server	(S)
Receiver	(R)
Setter/Target	●
Hitter	(H)
Digger	(D)
Player New Position	◌
Path of Player	⟶
Path of Ball	⇢

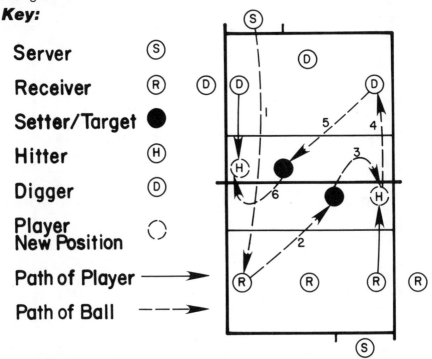

Explanation: Either server starts by serving to any receiver on the other side. The receiver passes to the setter, who sets to any one of the three receivers. The hitter spikes to the defense on the opposite side. If the defense digs the ball, then they attempt to counterattack. After an error, both sides rotate positions. The winning team initiates the next volley with a serve.

Variations:
1. Vary the task of the server with deep and short serves.
2. Train backward movement of the receivers by starting them at the three-meter line, then serving deep.
3. Start with the setter covering the spiker, then have all players cover.
4. Add the setter as a blocker against the attacker.

Cuban Coverage Drill
Contributor: Bob Gambardella
U.S. Military Academy

Purpose: To learn proper spiker coverage from service reception and transition.

Key:

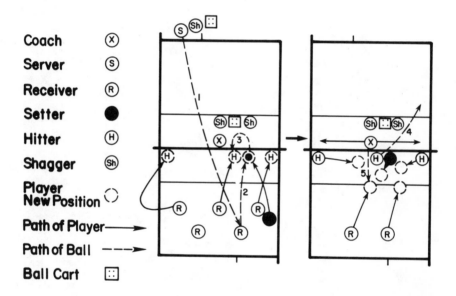

Coach	Ⓧ
Server	Ⓢ
Receiver	Ⓡ
Setter	●
Hitter	Ⓗ
Shagger	Ⓢₕ
Player New Position	◌
Path of Player	——→
Path of Ball	---→
Ball Cart	⬚

Explanation: The server serves to any area on the court. The setter penetrates and the receiver passes to the setter. The setter sets to position #2, #3, or #4, and the receiving team covers accordingly. The hitter spikes the ball and the coach tosses a ball over to the covering teammates, who try to play the ball up so that the setter can run the offense again. The drill can be continuous.

Variation:
1. After the receiving team passes the ball and the hitter spikes, the coach yells "Bump, Set, Spike" (medium tempo) so that the players can get to their defensive positions. The coach then spikes the ball into the court and the defense plays the ball up to the setter, who runs the offense. The hitter spikes the ball (the rest of the team covers) and the coach tosses the ball over so that the team (coverage) can play the ball up again to the setter.

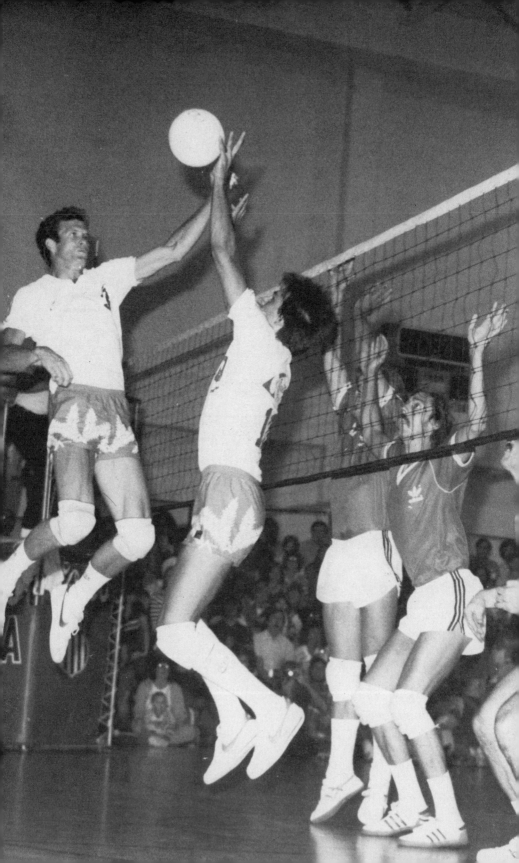

6

SIX-SKILL DRILLS

Two-Person Movement Drill
Contributor: Richard J. Scott
University of Montana

Purpose: To incorporate the following skills in a competitive situation: serve reception, spiking, setting, blocking, backcourt defense, and serving.

Key:

Server   (S)

Receiver   (R)

Blocker   (B)

Hitter   (H)

Digger   (D)

Setter/Target   ●

Path of Player ⟶

Explanation: The first server starts the drill. Play continues through the pass, set, spike, block, and dig. Once the ball is served, play stops only when the ball is dead. All players except setters rotate in pairs after hitters have put the ball away three times in a row. Setters stay in the same position but alternate every other pass.

Variations:
1. Include setters in rotation.
2. Rotate after every two plays.

Do It All Together

Contributor: Darlene A. Kluka
Texas Women's University

Purpose: To practice serve reception, offensive plays, and transition.

Key:

Coach	Ⓧ
Player	◯
Setter/Target	●
Server	Ⓢ
Digger	Ⓓ
Blocker	Ⓑ
Shagger	Ⓢʰ
Ball Cart	⬚

Explanation: The ball is served, and the receiving team passes and runs an offensive play against three blockers. If the ball is successfully attacked, the coach tosses a ball to the setter on the coach's side. The coach's team counterattacks with an offensive play. The receiving team, now in defensive position, defends against the attack and attempts to counterattack. The drill continues as long as the receiving team does not make an error. At the coach's discretion, a ball may be tossed to either one of the diggers on the coach's team to have them pass a free ball or down ball to the receiving team, who must adjust accordingly.

All-Court Initial Movement Drill

Contributor: John Blair
University of Tennessee

Purpose: To force quick initial transition movement; attending to what the opponent is doing.

Key:

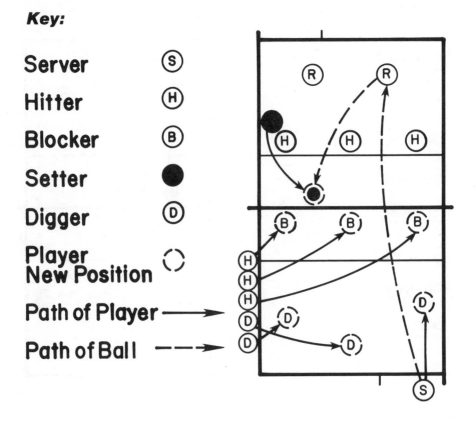

Server	Ⓢ
Hitter	Ⓗ
Blocker	Ⓑ
Setter	●
Digger	Ⓓ
Player New Position	◌
Path of Player	⟶
Path of Ball	⤏

Explanation: One side full serves to the receiving side. The serving team quickly moves to their respective defense positions. The receiving team passes and attacks. If the receiving team immediately ends play, they receive 1 point and the serve. If the serving team can keep the ball in play and counterattack, they receive 1 point and retain the serve. If either team fails to execute their initial play, they lose a point. Both teams start with 15 points. The drill continues until one team has lost all their points.

Side Out to Score Drill

Contributor: John Blair
University of Tennessee

Purpose: To instill the concept of playing to score points after siding out; to maintain intensity while serving.

Key:

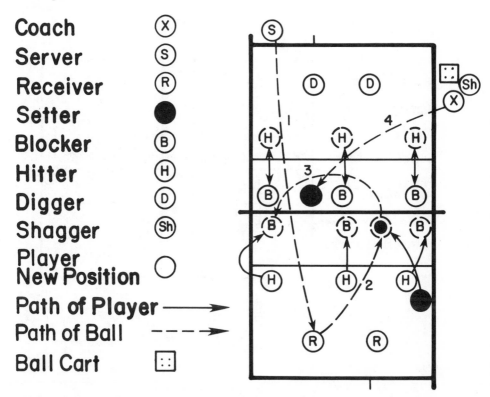

Coach   (X)
Server   (S)
Receiver   (R)
Setter   ●
Blocker   (B)
Hitter   (H)
Digger   (D)
Shagger   (Sh)
Player
New Position   ◯
Path of Player ⟶
Path of Ball   ---->
Ball Cart   ⊡

Explanation: A server serves to the opponent's reception formation. The receiving team attacks against no block. Regardless of the outcome, the receiving team immediately goes to defense. A ball is tossed by the coach to begin an automatic counterattack. The play then continues until one side wins the volley. If the receiving team wins, it is a side out and they can play for 1 point on the next ball, which is tossed to a player on the same side as the coach to initiate the volley. If the receiving team wins this volley, they score a point and are allowed to rotate, and the sequence begins again. The drill is continued until the receiving team scores 15 points.

INDEX OF DRILLS BY TYPE OF DRILL

ONE-SKILL DRILLS

Drill Name	Contributor	Drill Type	Pg. #
1. Accu-Speed Serving Drill	Bonnie Kenny	Multi-Rep Simple	10
2. Repeated Setting Drill	Ann E. Meyers	One Rep Simple	11
3. Bread and Butter Drill	Ralph Hippolyte	Multi-Rep Simple	12
4. Variable Spiking Drill	Mario Treibitch	One Rep Simple	13
5. Endurance Blocking Drill	Marilyn McReavy	Multi-Rep Simple	14
6. The Juggle Drill	Ed Halik	Multi-Rep Simple	15
7. Passing and Circuit Drill	Ralph Hippolyte	Multi-Rep Simple	16
8. Go For Two Drill	Bob Bertucci	Multi-Rep Simple	17
9. Dig and Roll Drill	Tina Bertucci	Multi-Rep Simple	18
10. The Great Chase Drill	Ann E. Meyers	Multi-Rep Simple	19

TWO-SKILL DRILLS

Drill Name	Contributor	Drill Type	Pg. #
1. Pass or Come Out to Serve Drill	Katrinka Jo Crawford	One Rep Combination	22
2. Receiving Carousel Drill	Frank Fristensky	One Rep Combination	23
3. Players vs. Coach Serve & Receive Drill	Tina Bertucci	One Rep Combination	24
4. Bread and Butter Attack Drill	Tina Bertucci	One Rep Combination	25
5. Find the Hitter Drill	Ralph Hippolyte	One Rep Combination	26
6. Continuous Dig and Set Drill	Tina Bertucci	One Rep Combination	27
7. 3 Corner Drill	Nancy Owen Fortner	One Rep Combination	28
8. Back Attack Drill	Barbara L. Viera	One Rep Combination	29

THREE-SKILL DRILLS

FOUR-SKILL DRILLS

FIVE-SKILL DRILLS

SIX-SKILL DRILLS

INDEX OF SKILLS

SERVING

DIGGING

BLOCKING

SERVICE RECEPTIONS

SETTING

SPIKING

INDEX OF CONTRIBUTORS

Six-Player Tip-Downball Drill

Contributor: John Blair
University of Tennessee

Purpose: To work on tipping, deep-court spiking, and tip-downball coverage.

Key:

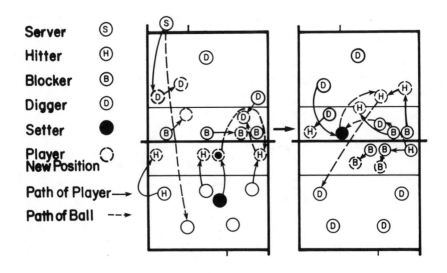

Explanation: The drill is similar to full-transition scrimmage, except that all balls that are set within the 3-meter line must be tipped. The same player may not tip to the same area of the court twice in succession. Any ball deeper than the 3-meter line may be attacked and the opposing team plays downball defense. Each player on the serving side serves two balls until all on the side have served. Repeat the drill with the other side serving. The game is played to 15 points, scoring 1 point each time a team wins a volley.